'I've always admired Jake and the way he's turned his pain into purpose. *The Comeback Code* is full of wisdom, and reflects Jake's big-hearted approach to learning from and through life.'

— Dr Lucy Hone, author of *Resilient Grieving*

# THE COMEBACK CODE

## The power of resilience when the going gets tough

JAKE BAILEY

ALLEN&UNWIN
AUCKLAND • SYDNEY • MELBOURNE • LONDON

First published in 2025



Allen & Unwin
Level 2, 10 College Hill, Freemans Bay
Auckland 1011, New Zealand
+64 (9) 377 3800
auckland@allenandunwin.com
www.allenandunwin.co.nz

83 Alexander Street
Crows Nest NSW 2065, Australia
+61 (2) 8425 0100

A catalogue record for this book is available from the National Library of New Zealand.

ISBN 978 1 991142 25 2

Design by Katrina Duncan
Printed and bound in Australia by the Opus Group

1 3 5 7 9 10 8 6 4 2

MIX
Paper | Supporting responsible forestry
FSC® C001695

For Scarlett and Will — who were children when this book was started and exceptional young adults by the time it was finished. I'm so proud to be your brother.

*If you can meet with Triumph and Disaster*
*And treat those two impostors just the same*
— from 'If' by Rudyard Kipling

# CONTENTS

# PREFACE

When I was seventeen, I thought the worst thing about meeting people was being asked, 'What do you want to do when you leave school?' Ten years on, I've figured out that there's something even worse than this: meeting people and immediately telling them about the time you had cancer.

A barista at a café a few years ago asked me, with a tone of surprise, 'Oh, have you been in a fight?' She'd spotted the mark below my right eye which, given the right lighting, looks as though I've copped a punch to the face and have a bit of a black eye and bruising around my cheekbone. In truth, the reason for the dark mark couldn't have been much further from her guess — it's from where I once had a cancerous tumour inside my face. When it grew rapidly it damaged the underlying structure of my cheek, then, as it shrank during my treatment, it left a bit of a hollow, which can cast a shadow that looks like a bruise.

But I don't generally throw this into conversations with strangers because, basically, that would be weird — so I laughed off her question with a 'No, nothing like that!'

'Hmmm, did you walk into a door?' she shot back.

'Nope, wasn't that either,' I replied, still trying to laugh it off.

'Did you fall down the stairs? Do you play rugby?'

After a few cycles of her guessing, and me laughing as I dismissed her guesses, I was becoming increasingly desperate to avoid having to tell her that the answer to the fun game she'd created was, well, cancer. Then she sealed our fate.

'Well, I'm not going to give you your coffee until I figure out how you've done that to yourself!' she announced. I could see it was going to be a long morning with no coffee, so I gave in.

'Well, I had cancer a couple of years ago, and . . .' I started.

The barista quite literally took a step backwards, her mouth dropped open in horror — and I got a free coffee.

So, let's get this out of the way up front: I'm Jake, I'm twenty-seven years old, and a few years ago I had the world's most aggressive form of cancer — but I'm all good now.

Hopefully, you don't feel weird that I told you about the whole cancer thing already. Please, don't feel like we're moving too fast. Yes, it happened pretty quickly — but that's not too far from normal for me. Pretty much all my conversations with people in everyday life — whether they're baristas, Uber drivers or people I sit next to on planes — quickly lead into me telling them about the time I got cancer and nearly died.

Let me be clear: that's not because I *want* to tell them — I'm not some kind of freak, I don't just go around blurting it out. Rather,

I end up telling them because what happened to me — my battle with cancer and my survival — is integral to everything about my life now: my job, my plans, my family.

Typically, it comes up because people ask what I do for work, and when I tell them I do public speaking, they want to know how I got into that. Sometimes it starts when they notice the tiny tattoo on the inside of my bicep — a line tally of the five years between when I was declared to be in remission (the cancer is probably gone but might come back) to when I was officially cured (cancer's gone, I win). Sometimes it's when they ask if I've been in a fight. But somehow, almost always, I end up telling people I've just met about the time I nearly died of cancer. It's like the world's worst superpower — a superhuman ability to make things awkward by bringing up cancer.

The thing is, for me, it's not awkward at all — it has been my life, my journey, my story or whatever else you might want to call it, so it doesn't make me feel uncomfortable or upset or afraid. It's more the impact which it has on other people. Most people treat cancer with a real sense of reverence or respect, which is perfectly fine, or it brings up feelings of fear or sadness because of their own experiences. But when I share my story with you here, I neither want nor expect you to feel that way about my story — because I certainly don't.

But we're here now, I've brought it up anyway, and it's actually integral to the rest of this book, so we'd best start off with the time I had cancer.

# 1

# THE WHOLE CANCER THING

The story begins back in 2015, around September. At the time, I was living a completely normal life for a teenager: I was eighteen years old, I was in year 13, and I was the senior monitor (or head boy) at my school. I was making a half-decent effort of my studies, playing a little sport (usually badly), partying with my mates and hanging out with my family on the weekends, planning what I was going to do the following year, and applying to universities and halls of residence. It was a completely normal, stock-standard teenage existence.

I was also dealing with my wisdom teeth coming through. They were hurting, but wisdom teeth *do* hurt, so that wasn't really a surprise. I went to my dentist and he took a scan of my jaw. He said that he could see a 'dark mark' on one side — not an infection of any kind, not a cyst or an abscess — he wasn't sure what it was, but he wasn't alarmed or worried by it. He referred me to a maxillofacial surgeon (a surgeon specialising in the mouth, jaw and face), and I made an appointment to get my wisdom teeth taken out about two months down the track.

But while I was waiting for that appointment, things started to go wrong in my body. First, the pain in my jaw started to get worse. It was an odd pain which would appear fairly suddenly, usually at night, then disappear just as suddenly after about an hour. Just for one hour, once a day. The pain started at the level of 'ouch, I've got toothache', but within a few weeks, the pain was reaching 'ho-ly shit, this is ridiculous' levels, just for that hour. I've broken bones before (see: 'played sport badly'), but this was beyond any pain I'd ever experienced. I would often pace around the house, very fast, because there was nothing else I could do to take my mind off the pain. Then it would suddenly stop, and I would sometimes cry from the relief.

More odd things began to happen. I started to randomly lose feeling in the lower half of my face — it would go completely, entirely numb. You know what it's like after you've had anaesthetic at the dentist and you've got no feeling in your lip? It seemed my body had decided that this was its new party trick, and it would whip out the numbness every now and then, for a few hours at a time — until one day, the feeling just didn't come back, and it stayed numb.

By this point, the pain in my jaw had got so bad that it stopped me from eating. I couldn't chew solid food at all. The solution? Vanilla UP&GO, and a lot of it. Two or three of the 1-litre bottles each day. Breakfast, lunch, and dinner? Vanilla UP&GO. Snack? Vanilla UP&GO. Funnily enough, despite drinking so much of it, somehow I actually still like it. (Surely there has to be a sponsored post in that.)

Throughout this time, perhaps unsurprisingly, I lost a lot of weight, and lost it quickly: 12 kilograms in about two weeks, gone. But hey, I was living on UP&GO, so I didn't think it was all that surprising.

I can almost picture your face right now, because I've seen people in audiences make that same face when I get to this part of my story during presentations. You must be reading all of this and thinking *what the hell? What on Earth were you doing?* The answer is that I was, initially, still living a very normal life: classes, sport, parties . . . to which you might think, what kind of idiot would have all this going on without thinking something was seriously wrong? I guess I didn't have the benefit of hindsight. I was going to a lot of medical appointments throughout this time — seeing two dentists, three maxillofacial surgeons, and I ended up going to A&E once or twice — and a very rational explanation was always provided for what I was experiencing. For most of the time, the doctors and dentists thought I must have an infection in my wisdom teeth. But in spite of the antibiotics and anti-inflammatories, I just kept getting sicker and sicker.

Things got more and more desperate. I went from being reasonably healthy, with odd, inconvenient bouts of pain and numbness, to being very thin and lethargic, to eventually, by the end of the term-three holidays, being incredibly sick. I could hardly get out of bed. I started to throw up blood. In less than two months I'd gone from 'ouch, my wisdom teeth hurt' to being admitted to hospital and finding out that, in fact, I was dying.

.........

I was admitted to hospital one evening, at the recommendation of one of the many doctors who was handling my weird, persistent dental problems. I was sent to a place called AMAU — the Acute Medical Assessment Unit in Christchurch Hospital, best described as 'the place where we put people who are sick but we don't know what is wrong with them yet'.

The first night I spent in AMAU was the first night I'd ever spent in a hospital, and I hardly slept. The beds were separated by thin curtains, and people groaned and moaned and suffered aloud all around me. The lady who was wheeled past at about 3 a.m., crying out loudly that she was dying, wasn't much of a welcoming party.

Over the coming days, the doctors did a whole variety of tests and procedures to try to figure out what was wrong with me: a CT scan, an MRI, an ultrasound, a gum biopsy (where they cut out a little piece of the gum to test it), a kidney biopsy (harder to cut a little bit out of a kidney, so they use a long, sharp, spiky thing and go in through your back), a bone-marrow aspirate (bone marrow is also hard to get to, because, well, it's inside your bones — so out comes another long sharp spike, which breaks straight through the bone and into the inside of your pelvis, to dig around and extract some marrow) and a spinal tap (a big needle stuck straight between your vertebrae and into your spinal column to suck out some fluid). It was a truly miserable few days.

All the while, I was getting sicker and sicker. The blood tests I was having three times a day showed that my kidneys were shutting down day by day, hour by hour. I now find it kind of funny when people say deep, philosophical things about how 'we're all dying — we're just dying very slowly'; well, that week, I was like the Usain Bolt of dying — I was dying really fast, faster than everyone else. Not instant, not immediate, not 'see you later' — but bit by bit, I was clocking out.

I lay in a hospital bed for days as the tests and scans went on. I now had pain in my legs, too — for about an hour at a time, just like the pain in my teeth, which was also getting worse and worse. It's hard to explain but the pain felt, impossibly, as though it was coming from *inside of the bones in my legs*. I've since been told that the cancer — which, as a blood cancer, was being produced by the marrow inside my bones — was reproducing so quickly that the cells could not be released into my bloodstream fast enough, so pressure was building up inside my bones, like a bottle of fizzy drink which has been shaken. As this pressure became greater and greater, my legs began to break from the inside out, developing microfractures, like a bottle about to explode. So the pain *was* coming from inside my bones after all.

This is when I started to realise that I was dying. As melodramatic as it sounds, my body simply knew. One afternoon, as I was being wheeled to a biopsy, the pain in my legs became so bad that I actually thought I was going to die at that very moment. It's impossible to really describe what it felt like, but perhaps you can imagine just how bad a pain must be for you to think that you are about to die, immediately, just because of it.

It started as an ache, then it built until it was unbearable, then it built until it couldn't possibly keep building, then it built some more. I writhed and cried and howled on the hospital gurney, and when I opened my eyes, I couldn't see anything. The whole world was white. I thought for a moment that this was the bright light you supposedly walk towards as you die, and I guess I thought I'd better let someone know, because I called out that I was dying. I had become that person who was wheeled past my bed at 3 a.m. only five nights earlier.

The doctors pushed some medication into the intravenous needle in my arm and I melted through the gurney and completely disappeared from the world around me. I woke up hours later back in my bed, still alive, but feeling less alive by the hour.

A day later, a doctor who I hadn't met before came into my hospital room and sat down beside my bed. She introduced herself as a haematologist, although I didn't have a clue what that was. She explained to me very slowly and very calmly that I had cancer — something called Burkitt non-Hodgkin lymphoma, the fastest-growing cancer known to man. It was stage four, and had been found in my brain lining, eye sockets, nasal passages, sinuses, gums, jaw, spinal fluid, pancreas and both of my kidneys. The cancer was so fast-growing, so aggressive that the tumours it was creating could double in size every twenty-four to forty-eight hours. Based on that, without treatment I had about two weeks left to live, and no guarantee of surviving even if I chose to have treatment. I had been spot on when I called out: I really was dying.

.........

So, you're eighteen, and you're told that you could be dead within two weeks.

You're told that everything you have been taught to strive towards since you were a child — the idea of having a nice house, and a nice family, and a good job — might never happen.

You're told that the next few months — the end of school, the leavers' dinner, the laughs, the parties, the classes, the lunches with mates — will never happen, because you'll be in a hospital bed, fighting for your life.

You're told everything that you assumed would always be yours, things which you believed could never be taken away from you, no matter how tough things got — like spending time with people you love and who love you — might no longer be yours to have either.

In short, you're told that your time is up. Not necessarily your entire life, but certainly the time when you had it pretty good in life — your teenage years, your youth, your normal life. Now you are in an arena, fighting the biggest battle you will ever fight, for the most valuable prize there is.

I want to make it really clear that I'm not so naïve as to think my story is special or unique or even uncommon. In fact, the complete opposite is true — many people enter that arena every day. Chances are that you will know someone who has been in that position. Maybe you have even been there yourself. But in some ways that's the problem. There are only a limited number of spaces available on the winning side — not everyone will make it through. In my case, I had an advantage — I was young and fit — but it certainly didn't feel like an advantage at the time.

Where do you go from here? Literally, what the hell comes next?

In my case, I went to a ward in Christchurch Hospital called the Bone Marrow Transplant Unit (BMTU) to do battle with the lymphoma.

While you're there, you see others battling around you. You see them, thin and frail, shuffling down the corridor, bald and gaunt, weak and sick, and undeniably, visibly, dying.

You're shocked by the sight of it, naturally. Perhaps you've seen someone before who was terribly sick, right at death's door, and you remember how it made you feel. It's more a reaction than an emotion: an intense discomfort. Except now you remember that's what *you* look like too, and that discomfort is what your friends and family feel when they come to see you.

It starts to feel pretty real when you figure out why the person from the room next door, who you were speaking to just the other day, has gone home and not come back to hospital.

Or when you look into the eyes of your parents, and see that what you're going through is killing them almost as much as it's killing you.

Or when you see nurses clad in masks and gloves and gowns carry a big bag labelled 'TOXIC' into your room, then hook it up so it can be pumped straight into your bloodstream. You know that, when it comes down to it, that bag contains your future, and any hope that you have of having one. One of those many bags contained the moment I am spending sitting here right now, typing this sentence. Another contained the laughs and stories I will share with friends tomorrow, another the precious moments I'll spend with my family next month. Every moment that you will ever have again, drip, drip, dripping into your arm.

It's at a time like this when, in my opinion, life is the most raw it can get. You are faced with the most pure pain, frustration and grief that exists, but also strength and wisdom, determination and fighting spirit. It absolutely and entirely fills that place. It coats the walls of the hospital ward, it coats the faces of friends and family members as they visit dying loved ones. It coats the inside of your sick bucket. When I arrived at the BMTU, I was placed in isolation, in a room that was entirely sealed off from the world using an airlock and filtered air system, because the chemotherapy treatment I was about to receive would devastate my immune system and leave me so vulnerable that even a little sniffle could kill me. My room was hidden away in the basement of the hospital — just down the corridor from the morgue. (Some of the other patients and I used to joke about how this had been done for convenience, which we thought was hilarious. I've since found out that other people who are *not* patients don't find that joke as funny as we did, but please feel free to laugh — there's nothing worse than a joke you really like falling flat.)

I spent the next fifty-two days straight in that room, leaving the hospital only once: to make my end-of-year speech as senior monitor at Christchurch Boys' High School. It was 29 October when I went into that room; it was December by the time I got to go home. It was early January when I finished treatment, and it was 29 January, three months to the day after my diagnosis, when one afternoon a doctor told me that I was now in remission: a fancy term for 'we can no longer find any cancer in your body'. That doesn't mean there is no cancer *there*, it just means that the doctors think the treatment has worked, so for now it can stop. They told me to go home, rebuild my body, try to rebuild my life, to have regular check-ups, to keep an eye out for any new symptoms, and to keep my fingers crossed that the cancer didn't come back.

End of story? Not even close.

# 2

# THE FOUR S MODEL

After being told by the doctors that I was in remission, I went back out into the world and started life again — and realised very quickly that I was not the same person I had been before cancer came barrelling into my life.

This isn't supposed to be some massive, shocking revelation — you'd probably find it more surprising if I told you that going through all of this *hadn't* changed me in some huge way. But what you might not have been expecting is that I realised that my life was *far better* after the cancer than it had been before.

In short, I was now a happier, more grateful person, who was less worried about people, less worried about the small things, less worried about the future. I suppose the easiest way to sum it up is that my life after the cancer *just felt better* than it had been beforehand.

I found this pretty confusing, because if you just looked at the facts, my life was a whole lot *worse* than it had been before the cancer.

For starters, as a result of my treatment I had been left with a condition called peripheral neuropathy. It's pretty much like how in the case of a broken neck or back leading to a spinal-cord injury, the messages can no longer get through from the brain to parts of the body and you can be left paralysed. I had this same issue as a result of nerve damage caused by my chemotherapy. In practice, this meant that my legs had stopped doing what I told them to, so I was stuck in a wheelchair or on crutches. I couldn't even roll myself over in bed at night, so I had to get my girlfriend to help me. I couldn't walk up and down the stairs at home, so I had to sit and slide myself up or down them. I couldn't play sport, or go to my part-time job that I loved, or go out to do things with mates without it being inconvenient at the very least. To top this all off, the doctors told me there was no treatment for this type of nerve damage, so the only option was to wait it out and hope that things improved — but I did need to prepare myself for the possibility that I would not walk unassisted ever again.

The second reason that my life should not have felt better was that this whole remission thing, while far better than having cancer, was a long way from being great. The doctors told me that, for now, I was fine — but in their experience, there was a 25–35 per cent chance the cancer would come back in the next five years. If it did, my chances of surviving were not brilliant: if my treatment had not worked the first time, it was unlikely to work the second. So, in addition to potentially being unable to walk again, I now had a risk of relapse hanging over my head for the next five years.

But in spite of the fact that my life seemed objectively to be so much worse than it had been before cancer, it actually felt so much better. Even with these issues to face, I was now much happier than I had been a year earlier without them. To me, that made no sense at all. Why did my life now not feel as bad as it should, let alone better than it had before?

The answer to that question was that through the cancer, through that hardship and adversity, I had gained a whole lot of *resilience*.

## Why Resilience?

A few years ago, I was asked to give an address at a service in the Christ Church Cathedral (well, its temporary cardboard replacement). The dean was very open-ended on what I could speak about: my brief was something along the lines of 'fifteen minutes on a topic which is a passion of yours'. So I sat down to sketch out a few notes on what I might cover in my talk, and immediately came up against a problem.

> . . . a topic which is a passion of yours.

To put it bluntly, throughout my life — in fact, until very recently — I've never really had a passion. Some of my peers at school excelled in sports, to which they dedicated themselves completely. Others had one class for which they had some natural, inbuilt talent and interest — which meant they would generally end up proof-reading my assignments for that subject. I had friends who were passionate about, and really good at, breakdancing, skiing, luging, horse-riding, ice hockey, cooking . . .

Me, on the other hand? I was, well, I would say a jack of all trades, master of none. I suspect my mates would put it something more along the lines of 'pretty useless at most stuff'. It wasn't that I was apathetic or lazy, and it's not that I wasn't good at some things, but I felt like I was lacking a sole passion or prevailing talent, like those around me often had.

After my cancer in 2015, journalists would find it incredibly difficult to add background information about me to their reports. My family and I have a running joke about one particular news item which referred to me as having been a keen and naturally talented football player prior to my cancer diagnosis — which couldn't have been further from the truth. I was the goalkeeper for the Fifth XI, the school's social soccer team, and that was only because I was too uncoordinated to just use my feet — I needed to be able to use my hands as well.

But on the day I received the email from the dean of Christ Church Cathedral, I was in a cabin in Arthur's Pass, having just finished the first day of the Coast to Coast, a truly gruelling multisport endurance event comprising 243 kilometres of running, cycling, kayaking and hurting from the west coast of the South Island to the east. It's one of a number of endurance events I have taken on over the past few years — a choice which usually gets a confused 'why?' from most people I tell about it. Why would you do that? Why would you deliberately put yourself through all that suffering?

The answer to that question, and the topic I centred my speech at the cathedral around, is that it is my passion. Not the sport, and not the suffering, but rather, my passion is something you can only experience *through* suffering — and that is *resilience*. My passion is resilience.

I don't know how my friends found their passions in life. I once had a mate who took up the bagpipes because his parents insisted that he play an instrument and, in an effort to get back at them, he chose the loudest and most annoying one he could think of. Other mates were guided into a sport or art by their parents, and found that they loved it. For me, I happened to stumble across my passion by getting cancer.

Chemotherapy does lots of funny things to your body. There are lots of side effects: it makes your hair fall out, it makes your eyebrows and eyelashes fall out, you lose a lot of weight — I lost over 15 kilograms. The tips of my fingers went numb and my legs stopped working for a bit. There's a fair bit of throwing up, although we don't have to talk about that in detail. But undoubtedly, the greatest side effect of chemo for me was developing resilience.

Why was this so fantastic? Why do any of us need resilience?

The answer is what psychologists call 'inevitable adversity'. It's the idea that, no matter what you do, at some stage things are going to go wrong in your life. Not that suffering or failure *might* happen; or that it will happen to you only if you are bad; or that it will happen to someone more unfortunate, or somewhere else; or that — and this one is important — you can somehow avoid it, through cleverness or luck. (I'm the expert on this one: I was never going to be the teenager who got cancer — I always gave my gold-coin donation for Canteen on non-uniform days, and isn't that an insurance policy against getting cancer? Turns out it doesn't really work like that.) Instead:

> Inevitable adversity is the reality that, during the course of your life, some pretty rough things are going to happen to you.

To put that idea into less fancy words, it's accepting that you basically spend the whole time you're on this Earth trying to fix shit that has gone wrong. Sometimes more shit happens, sometimes less. Sometimes it's big shit, sometimes it's minor. Sure, there will be amazing, exciting, brilliant experiences along the way . . . but always, consistently, *forever*, there will be things going wrong which you'll have to overcome. These things going wrong are what we call adversity.

I get that this sounds awful, but I swear that it isn't a bad thing at all, for a whole range of reasons. Sometimes, the bad things which happen will actually leave you with positive upsides, or good memories, or funny stories. Sometimes they leave you a better person. Sometimes things which you thought were bad turn out to have been good in hindsight. For me, getting cancer ticks all of those boxes.

And even when the bad things actually are *just bad things*, without any positive outcome or silver lining, they're still entirely unavoidable. Life is not a smooth road for any of us, nor is it meant to be. Things *will* go terribly wrong in all of our lives

— at different times, and of different severities, undoubtedly. But still, this adversity is entirely expected and normal. It's literally *just part of life*.

The bottom line is that some degree of suffering is an ordinary part of being a human being and hanging out on Earth. Occasionally your life will veer unexpectedly off the path that you were on — a path which you quite liked — onto another path which you don't like so much. Losing, failing, falling, and the suffering that comes from those experiences — all of this is a necessary and even positive part of the experience of being human.

Aside from this idea of inevitable adversity, of things going wrong sometimes, the reality is that *everything* in life is hard to some degree, and often your choices are simply based on *what is less hard*. For example, running is hard, but so is being called chubby by other kids. I know, because I've dabbled in both. Studying persistently to get good results is hard, but so is failing exams. Making sacrifices to pursue an amazing opportunity is hard, but so is standing by and passing up a dream. Failing in the pursuit of a goal is hard, but so is never knowing what you might have achieved had you given it a go.

That said, we'd all rather be happy as often as we possibly can, rather than spending the whole time battling through, right? So, if we can't do much about the 'bad things will happen' side of the equation, what is there left to work with?

> How do we overcome these events, and make the best of the only opportunity that we have to give life a crack?

Well, thankfully, as humans we have *resilience*: this incredible ability to overcome and successfully cope with negative emotions and situations, and to recover from things going wrong. Bad things are going to happen, so the only option available to us is our *response and reaction* to these difficult situations.

If we can cope successfully with the adverse things which will almost certainly happen to us in life, like losing our parents, or having our heart broken, or having a medical event happen to us or someone we love, or just getting through life's everyday challenges, then we will be okay. If, on the other hand, we fall and suffer and struggle to recover each time one of these incidents occurs, then our life will be one long, protracted suffer-fest.

If you struggle to deal with and overcome things that go wrong — be they big things or just day-to-day small things — you're going to always be on the back foot, always trying to recover. If, on the other hand, you're quite good at doing this, you give yourself a bit more time to look around and enjoy the journey. In other words, how 'good' your life is or how happy it makes you is directly tied, not to the adversity which happens to you in your life, but rather *how successfully you're able to weather it.*

That is what resilience is: the ability to overcome the challenging things which happen to you. Therefore, it's effectively a way to determine how happy you will be in life.

> This is what had happened to me through cancer, and this was why my life felt better afterwards, even though it should have felt so much worse: as a result of going through this significant adversity, and learning the skills

> and tools I needed to get through, I was now a whole lot more successful at overcoming and facing other challenges in my life. Whereas previously I had been weighed down worrying about things like exam results, or other people's opinions of me, or the future, I now had a framework that allowed me to think my way through these everyday challenges, and as a result I was now more effective, more efficient at facing the things which go wrong for all of us — not only the big stuff, the life-and-death stuff, but the things which we all face, each and every day. Thanks to that, my life now felt a whole lot better than before.

A good life is, of course, a life of happiness. As humans, we seek happiness through doing things we enjoy, like spending time with family and friends, or going on holidays, or helping others, or, sometimes, through accumulating possessions. But I believe that this mindset teaches us an incorrect definition of happiness: that happiness is an outcome or a result, something we *achieve*. Rather, I believe that happiness is a skill, and like any skill it can be developed or practised — and fortunately, there is a surprisingly simple formula for doing so.

The way to create happiness is simply to be *as good as you possibly can at recovering when things go wrong*. No matter what happens to us, good or bad, how happy a life we have will be decided in the majority by how good we are at utilising this one skill — far more so than how much money we have or don't have, how good or how poor our health is, or how many times we fall and fail. What will inevitably decide how favourably you look back on your life is simply *how good you became at bouncing back from the things which went wrong, rather than how many things went wrong or how big they were.*

Maybe you think this is genius, maybe you think I sound completely insane — either way, I can't take all of the credit or blame, because this isn't just something I've dreamt up all on my own.

> Research shows us that the happiest and most successful people in life are not the most intelligent, or skilled, or fortunate, or gifted, but rather those who are the most resilient.

Makes sense, right? It doesn't matter how well you're positioned to achieve big things in life if you fall over at the first hurdle and aren't able to get back up again. This concept of being able to overcome bad things doesn't only allow you to be happier; it is critical to how much you achieve in your time on Earth.

If you're anything like me, you will have realised by now (as I did, while lying in my hospital bed) that getting some of this resilience stuff is pretty much essential. As I was going through my treatment, I realised that it would be pivotal, not only for my survival and recovery from cancer, but in everything that went wrong in life from that day onwards — from the cat dying to stubbing my toe on the bedframe.

And so began for me what has been a nine-year obsession with the idea of resilience: where to find it, whether it can be taught (and if so, how to teach it), who has it and who doesn't, *why* some people have it and some don't, what creates and what reduces it, and what it means for someone's happiness and success in life. For the past nine years, I've been lucky enough to have had the chance to speak to more than 100,000 people across nearly a dozen countries: in over a hundred schools and to audiences from a huge variety of backgrounds, countries and cultures, ranging from professional sportspeople to prisoners; from kids in outback towns to the CEOs of some of the world's biggest companies; and from people in retirement homes to officials from foreign governments — all with the aim of trying to figure out how best we can equip people with the skills to allow them to overcome life's challenges, to become more resilient.

I don't share my story because I like to tell people all about how I got cancer. I share my story because I hope that some of the lessons I learnt along the way, particularly those which relate to how we can become more resilient, can be beneficial to other people facing their own challenges in life, whatever those challenges might be.

## The Four S Model in Action

I'm far from certain that I've got it all figured out, but there are some bits I do know for sure. These facts are derived from a combination of what I've learnt in my own life and experiences, what I've learnt from interviewing people, what I've learnt from studying positive psychology, and what I've learnt from experts who study resilience as their job. There are three big things:

- Resilience is, undoubtedly, the most critical factor to having a happy and successful life.
- Resilience is particularly essential to learn early in life, before you get too far out into the world where, when things go wrong, they tend to go *really* wrong.
- Resilience can be learnt and strengthened.

This means it is within our power as a society to set up young people to go out into the world and succeed, through being able to bounce back from anything bad that happens to them.

The way that I teach these skills and tools is something called the Four S Model: four things all beginning with the letter S, which cancer has taught me, which made me more resilient and a better person, and which if applied to your life can do the same for you.

Four things which are supported by studies, research and evidence, and which we know for a fact make people better at getting through tough times.

Four bits of knowledge and advice that I collected along the way, from four separate points of the same story.

Four strategies without which I don't think I would've got through the cancer.

Four things I would go through cancer again to learn all over again.

Four things which, above all, I hope other people can learn themselves — without having to go through cancer.

**Those four things are:**

1. **Slow Down:** don't fall into the trap of facing adversity as one big challenge and becoming overwhelmed by it — instead, break the challenge into manageable chunks.
2. **Salvage:** deliberately seek out the good within the bad — no matter how creative you have to be.
3. **Streamline:** try to minimise and contain the everyday fears and anxieties which we all have.
4. **Stand Alongside:** maximise the impact of community and support on your ability to outlast and survive adversity.

To be clear, it wasn't the cancer itself which gave me any of these things. Cancer doesn't come with a magical handbook of life lessons, and the keys to a better future are not hidden in the bottom of the bags of chemotherapy drugs. I didn't sit in the hospital ward and have D&Ms with the other patients about the meaning of life which left me feeling enlightened. The only reason these changes have occurred for me is that going through the cancer and the harrowing treatment — going through that *adversity* — taught me a whole bunch of skills, tools and strategies for surviving tough times.

Getting through that particular significant adversity showed me ways to become more effective at getting through *all* adversity on a day-to-day basis, be it minor or major. This gives me a lot more time in my life to focus on the good stuff and that which makes me happy. It makes me better at getting through the tough times, so I can carry on my journey more comfortably and easily. It gives breathing room to enjoy life.

The lessons in resilience included in this book won't all come from me, but also from a range of successful and wise young people — champions of resilience and success who have been generous enough to share their own stories and talk about what they learnt along the way. All of them have overcome mighty challenges, challenges made small only in comparison with their subsequent successes, as well as the same challenges that most of us face as we grow up. There will also be science and research and empirical evidence around resilience, but not so much that it'll bore you out of your mind — just enough to give you confidence that what you are reading is true and not some nonsense that I've dreamt up. And there are a few other stories mixed in there — because hey, maybe I've got a few good stories other than just the time I got cancer.

Hopefully, there will be a line or two which will make it worth the time you spend sifting through these pages — something that really hits home for you, and makes you think differently, and helps you to become more resilient. But if nothing else, I hope it serves as proof that there are others who have walked the same path as you — through challenges, to success.

# 3

# SLOW DOWN

In July 2019, thirty-two teenage inmates at a juvenile justice facility in New South Wales started a riot. They cornered a guard, took their keys, gained access to a shed which held grounds-keeping supplies and armed themselves with chainsaws. Then they took over the facility and trashed it. Eventually they climbed onto the roof, where they taunted the riot police who would ultimately arrest them. The riot went on for twenty-one hours.

Less than a year earlier, I had walked into that same facility to present to many of these kids, educating them about resilience.

The young prisoners I worked with were in there for serious stuff — this wasn't a place you ended up because you'd gone off the rails a little. You might think you know the kind of people who end up in a place like this. You might know people who reckon they're pretty tough. You don't, and they aren't. I remember one of the guards who escorted me through the building saying, 'You don't end up in here for taking chocolate bars, or anything much short of a life.'

The prison itself was quite similar to what you see on TV. The officers' keys do jingle with every step, the doors do make that buzzing noise when they open and that clanging noise when they close, and people do yell out from cells. The biggest difference is that when you think prison, you probably think bars, but you'd be wrong. Modern prisons have a lot of metal doors with small Perspex windows, and not a lot of bars.

You've probably also got a vision in mind right now of what the kids in this place look like. I did, too. But when I got there, I was shocked to see these young people were virtually indistinguishable from all the other regular teenage guys I had spent my school years surrounded by. A few of them had face or neck tattoos, but most of them looked and acted like very average, very normal, even rather upstanding young men. They looked me in the eye and shook my hand, and in that moment I could just as easily have been meeting them on the sideline at a school rugby game. These guys didn't wear a label with their crimes written on it, and the guards weren't allowed to give even a hint of why they were in there.

It messed with me for weeks afterwards, as I tried to make sense of the likeability and charisma of many of these young guys, weighed up against the faceless victims of their unknown crimes. If you were related to one of their victims, you probably would want nothing more than to hate, despise and punish these inmates for what they had done. But in my case, I just got on with speaking to them.

The main thing about prison which I still can't wrap my head around is the timeframe. Let's be clear here: going to prison is a pretty massive adversity. Regardless of whether someone deserves it, or deserves something even worse, there's no denying that going to prison is a time of serious adversity for that person. Some of these kids knew that they were going to be locked up for nearly as many years as they had been alive. They were facing a dozen or more years, day after day, week after week, month after month, having no freedom to leave, no freedom to decide what they did with their day, no freedom to live a normal life like almost everyone else their age. They had committed crimes and were being punished for them — but I can't even begin to imagine what that must be like, looking at nearly the same number of years you've been on this Earth now being the same number of years of jail time ahead of you.

I can't even think much further than a year ahead without my brain starting to hurt, let alone knowing I'd have years and years of living the same restricted, constrained life ahead of me. It must be impossible to comprehend — or maybe it is possible to comprehend but impossible to face, and maybe that's why they rioted that day.

On the day I spoke to them, one of the boys put his hand up and asked me how I had dealt with my diagnosis, knowing what a long and tough road I had ahead of me. Maybe he was also struggling to make sense of what was ahead of him. The answer, I told him, was the first of the Four Ss: Slow Down.

•••••••••

In some ways, being given my cancer diagnosis was a bit like being sent to prison. Obviously, while I was 'doing my time' I received amazing care from the staff, my family and friends, but there were definitely some parallels.

Physically, there was the confinement to a single space. Once I began my treatment, I went into my room on the ward and stayed there for the next fifty-two days straight, unable to leave because of my compromised immune system. Trapped in that room, I lived by the hospital's schedule, waking and sleeping and having medicine and check-ups and scans and human contact as and when the rules dictated.

Then there was the time aspect: from the outset of my diagnosis, I knew it wasn't going to be an easy fix. It's worth noting that actually, by cancer standards, my treatment was exceptionally quick — I underwent only three months of treatment, whereas many patients go through years. I've met seven-year-old kids facing four years of chemotherapy. I was incredibly fortunate that my treatment was so short, but at the same time it was far from a brief exercise, or at least it certainly felt that way. And there was nothing I could do to speed up this process, no way to make time go faster. There was also nothing I could do to escape it, no compromise I could make, no way out of the current reality, and no real end point in sight. I was on board a roller coaster, and the carriage had started rolling away from the platform.

Except for the physical confinement, all of these things are hallmarks of significant adversity in general: a situation you find yourself in where there's no escape from that reality, where you can't make time pass any faster or speed up the process, where you just have to be able to wait and outlast the suffering. Whether it's the tumultuous period after a break-up, or getting through your end-of-year exam block, or going to jail, or getting cancer, there will be periods of adversity you'll face in life where your only option is to hold tight and wait for things to blow over. Sometimes, like in the case of the loss of a loved one, there is no 'end' in sight to hang on for.

How can you get through something so significant, something you have no knowledge of how to overcome, something there's no guidebook for, something that might not have even a finish line, something which is now the new normal, something which is permanent and inescapable?

> You can't change it, fix it, undo it or repair it . . . you can only outlast it.

A big part of being a teenager is being pushed to look ahead, into the future, all the time. When it comes to high school, you're always being encouraged to think five or even ten years ahead. You have to pick certain subjects one year to be able to do them the following year, to be able to get university entrance or an apprenticeship, so you can then go on to get the job you want for the rest of your life. Sometimes it seems like all anyone ever asks you is who and what you want to be when you're older. And the whole time, you will wish you were a few years older: first you want to stay up past 10 p.m., then you want to get your licence, then move out of home. Because of this mixture of encouragement to focus on the future, and knowing that some of life's most exciting experiences are tantalisingly close yet just out of reach, you can become pretty accustomed to always looking ahead.

The issue with this — and what I think plays a part in our youth mental-health crisis — is that *when it comes to adversity, trying to look into the future is one of the worst things you can do*. We know this from research and scientific studies — people who take a long-term perspective or consider a long-term timeframe during adversity don't do so well. Particularly when it comes to significant adversity, taking the whole problem or issue as one big problem, and looking at the horrible big picture all at once, is a recipe for being entirely overwhelmed and crushed by the weight of it all. If you make it look so big it's insurmountable, it often will be.

At the beginning of my cancer journey, if I had looked at the hundred or so days of treatment ahead of me — the chemotherapy and the horrific medical procedures I was going to go through — it would have felt like an impossible mountain to conquer. I don't know how I would've got through it, or even if I would've got through it at all. I wonder sometimes — and I'm not afraid to admit that I don't know the answer — whether I would've wanted to have even tried.

If the doctor, at the outset of my treatment, had showed me a 'highlights reel' of the next few months — the bone-marrow aspirates, the lumbar punctures, the way I would get so skinny that I would have to put a pillow between my legs when I lay on my side in bed because otherwise the bones in my withered legs would knock together, the times I would throw up so violently that my ears would ring for hours afterwards, the times I would get so weak that I couldn't sit up for more than fifteen minutes at a time, even with the bed raised behind me — I don't know if I would have, or *could have*, agreed to go through it all.

But I did, and because of that I now know that, faced with the same choice, I would and I could survive it. Still, part of me wonders if my eighteen-year-old self, who had never fully tested his resilience, would have felt the same way if he had really known what lay ahead. I like to think so, given the alternative, but I'll never know for sure.

Luckily for me, no one did show me a highlights reel of what was to come. In fact, I had the absolute opposite experience. At the start, the reality of cancer treatment was still just as vague and unfamiliar to me as it hopefully is for you. I had no idea what would come the day after my diagnosis, or on day one of my treatment, or on any other day after that.

The first few days of my diagnosis sounded like: 'Right, we're going to put a PICC line in your arm now', 'Now we need to take a scan of your heart to check that it's healthy before we give you any chemotherapy', 'Now we're going to give you some of these drugs to help prepare your body for treatment' and so on. There was no to-do list for me to check off, particularly in the early stages, but it would've been as long as my arm if there had been one. I didn't have time to worry about what tomorrow might hold, because I was too busy signing paperwork to enable my blood transfusions. I didn't have time for worrying about what it meant to get a PICC line put into my arm, because I was busy getting my chest shaved for an ECG on my heart.

In the early days after my diagnosis, this attitude came naturally — I had to adopt the mindset of taking things as they came, because there was no other choice. I didn't know what the overall plan was, or even if there was one; there was only life by the hour, because once one hour was up, I'd be meeting a new doctor with a new area of expertise in a new ward. There was no overall concept of 'beating cancer', no 'overcoming it', no 'fight': there was just getting through one thing, then dealing with the next, then the next. But instead of this all feeling overwhelming or stressful, it actually felt the opposite — it was a steady, gradual process, and the focus being on right now instead of what's next put my mind at ease. And this was the way I came to find the first S: Slow Down.

.........

Once the treatment really got started, things were a bit more predictable. The doctors would give me a rundown on what was scheduled: the plan for exactly what chemo I would be having, on what days, for my next treatment cycle, which was twenty-eight days. It was like getting the worst study planner ever — a study planner where you also knew you'd be stuck in one room for almost every hour of every day. And every time you did some study, you wanted to throw up a little bit.

This was really when Slowing Down started to come into its own. If there was ever a moment to go '*Oh shit!*' while looking at the path ahead of me, it was then, when I could see my chemo, my lumbar punctures and other procedures, what lay immediately ahead, well mapped out. At every point, every day, the road ahead just looked bleak.

The worst part was, all this was the best-case scenario! I had to hope that these next twenty-eight days of my treatment were as bad as planned, because the only reason they could be any easier or different from the schedule would be if:

1. I had died.
2. My treatment had been deemed hopeless and I was moved to palliative care, i.e. I was about to die; or
3. I was responding very poorly to the treatment due to a rare side effect or something, so my treatment protocol had changed — which would mean I was no longer getting the most effective treatment.

I had to be hopeful, and grateful, that my next twenty-eight days would be as bad as they were expected to be.

If I wanted to look beyond the next twenty-eight days, there was an even bigger mountain of adversity ahead. From the moment my haematologist told me I had cancer, I knew I had nearly a hundred days of chemotherapy and gruesome medical procedures ahead of me. And then, if that went perfectly — if I was incredibly lucky, and made it through that largely in one piece — then I had five years of the risk of relapse, of the cancer coming back, hanging over my head. So really, I was being told that, best-case scenario, I had a fairly rough five-and-a-bit years ahead of me.

There were two ways I could tackle this. I could've wrestled with the big picture, tried to look ahead to a time beyond cancer, tried to strive to get to that future, tried to pull away from the adversity — but what would be the benefit of that? Would it change the situation? Or would it just crush me under the weight of how unachievable it all felt?

Instead, as I went through my treatment, every day I would deliberately, wilfully ignore the fact that there was going to be more chemotherapy tomorrow, and the day after that, and the day after that. Instead, I focused on getting through *just that day's chemotherapy*. Somehow, that made it all seem bearable. I would tick it off, one bag of chemo at a time, one horrible procedure at a time, one day at a time, focusing only on each individual step in the treatment journey. Never tomorrow, never next week, never the next cycle.

This is, at its core, the idea of Slowing Down — to deliberately, consciously stop rushing into the future, to take things day by day and, where possible, avoid getting fixated on the overall picture of the situation you find yourself in. To concentrate your focus on getting through whatever you can manage — be it a day, a week, a month at a time. Because in times of adversity there are very few — if any — scenarios where you're going to feel better considering the adversity as a whole, rather than focusing on tackling it in bite-sized, more manageable pieces.

........

I need to be up front in saying that this concept of Slowing Down, or taking things one day at a time, is far from my own personal invention. It's effectively a strategy which psychologists call chunking: breaking down a bigger goal, or target, or adversity, into smaller 'chunks', and taking them on one at a time, rather than as a whole. They recommend it because . . . well, because it works. We know that doing so effectively allows you to trick your brain into believing things are more bearable.

I said earlier how people who face adversity as one big challenge, in one big lump, have worse outcomes — that's in comparison to people who take things bit by bit and break them up into more manageable chunks. If you google it, you'll find a million articles by psychologists employing a million awful metaphors to describe it: 'a masterful painting is made up of many small strokes' and 'how do you eat an elephant? One bite at a time' and so on. No matter how you dress it up, though, psychologists have been encouraging people to use this technique for a range of issues for a long time now.

Breaking challenges up into chunks is also not my exclusive idea because, well, we already do it naturally — it's human instinct. Whether it's breaking a run down into kilometre blocks, or breaking an assignment into paragraphs or sections of a word count, or breaking an end goal into a series of targets, or breaking cooking down into steps, we all apply 'chunking' every day, deliberately or not. As I said above, no one specifically taught me to 'chunk' my cancer treatment, no one encouraged me to think this way. It wasn't a conscious strategy at the time — it was just how my mind adapted to the situation I found myself in. And this underlines how it can be one of the most effective ways of coping with adversity: breaking it up into smaller elements and tackling them one by one. When times are tough, chunking, or Slowing Down, is an incredibly powerful tool.

It's what your brain is hardwired to do, but unfortunately, in times of stress and adversity, sometimes the brain gets short-circuited and doesn't do its job — which is unfortunate, because the times when you feel overwhelmed are when you need to employ it the most. During times of adversity, some of the neurochemicals released in response to stress can effectively shut down the part of your brain which perceives time. You might have experienced that feeling when something has gone catastrophically wrong. The first sensation is like you are stuck in a moment which is never going to end or that time seems to have slowed down. Often, it's accompanied by a sense of overwhelm or thinking, 'How on Earth am I going to get through this?'

This is when consciously Slowing Down comes into play, enabling you to take the next step forward, to continue moving and not be completely bowled over by the situation you find yourself in. It's applicable to adversity of any sort, big or small, but it works best on large, complex problems. Rather than being daunted by the magnitude of the overall problem or its solution, you can start looking at the issues within the adversity individually and tackle them as such, getting through them piece by piece, day by day.

All Black Will Jordan, whose interview you'll read at the end of this chapter, reflected on this when he was waiting for more information about his migraine condition. At the time, he wasn't sure how serious it was, whether it could be cured or if it would end his career:

> 'The days when I was sitting there not feeling great and I was spiralling — thinking about different treatments and the risks; maybe I hadn't heard from the specialist in a while; maybe I'd had a training day and felt awful, so what's this going to mean? — as soon as I got into that state of mind I started to feel a lot worse. I did a lot of work with [All Blacks mental skills coach] Gilbert Enoka around shortening my horizons — instead of looking a month into the future, I would say, 'Okay, I've got a session every day for the next four days, let's get through that.' Or, 'I've got a meeting with my neurologist on Monday, let's just focus on that.' When you start looking too far into the long term, there's so much uncertainty, so much worry in that. If you don't have something to train your mind on, it starts going in all sorts of different places. Taking a day-to-day perspective, that was huge for me.'

Some students tell me that they found themselves using this approach a lot during the Covid pandemic, when there was no end in sight and no clarity around what would happen in the future — or even when we would no longer be confined to our homes. In those times, the natural coping response for a lot of people was to focus on what they could control on a day-by-day basis — getting some exercise, completing work online, staying in touch with friends from a distance — taking it step by step instead of trying to focus on what the next week, month or year might hold, because at that time no one knew. This is often what adversity feels like.

.........

The first strategy really is as simple as this: when things aren't going well or you are facing adversity, don't fall into the trap of applying the teenage mindset of thinking a year, or five years, or ten years ahead, and feeling overwhelmed by it all. While being forward-thinking is such a natural part of this time of your life, it's also the absolute worst lens to view adversity and challenges through. Constantly taking in the big picture and considering the whole of the challenge ahead of you will leave you with no clear next step to take, and the risk that you will be overcome by that overwhelming sense of dread that can come from being confronted by massive adversity.

Usually in life, there won't be a shortcut through or a fast-forward button for whatever you're facing — whether it's your teenage years, your cancer treatment or (hopefully not) your time in prison. There's just another day, another challenge, another problem ahead of you — but recognising that, and taking each hurdle as it comes, is infinitely more manageable than facing the collective sum of all these challenges put together. If you take them individually, and deal with each one as best you can, then the next step to take will become clear.

The alternative is being crushed by the weight and magnitude of the adversity facing you, as I suspect I would have been in hospital if it weren't for Slowing Down. Being able to face challenges one by one is absolutely critical to getting through — to being resilient.

## Summary

- When you're staring up at the mountain, try to plot out just the next bit of the route. You don't need to see the whole path to the summit, only the best way to start and the first steps you'll take.
- Slow down, and take it one day at a time. This is not a cop-out, nor is it shying away or ignoring the truth of the situation. It's the same thing I did during day after day of chemo — just get through the next thing ahead of you, then the next, until the adversity has been overcome or has reached a manageable state.

## Will Jordan — Finding Motivation from Within

Will Jordan is an All Black, World Rugby Breakthrough Player of the Year 2021, and an all-round top guy. I know the first two things because his name is pretty hard to miss if you've given even a passing glance to the sports news over the past few years. I know the last one because Will and I went through school together and were monitors (as prefects were called at our school) in our final year. I like to say I played a lot of rugby against him, which is half true — the rugby was played on a PlayStation in the monitors' common room. I don't seem to recall ever beating him at even that.

Will's name has come up at a few presentations I've given in recent years, when someone in the audience makes the connection that we went to the same school at about the same time, and asks if I knew him. I'm stoked to say that not only did I know Will at school, but he was one of the people who really pulled through when I was in hospital: one of a few guys who I'd been friendly with but not exceptionally close to during the school year, but who fully had my back when times were at their shittiest. He, and they, had no obligation to go above and beyond to offer exceptional support — and they still did. Even at that time, distracted as I was by my treatment, his kindness really struck me, and it still sticks with me now.

Despite that, I now vigorously try to avoid talking about Will when I'm speaking at schools, because last time I admitted to knowing him the next two questions from the audience were:

'Do you have Will Jordan's phone number?' and 'Can we call Will Jordan right now?'

When I sat down to chat with Will for this book, he was two weeks back into playing rugby at a professional level after a migraine-related condition had kept him off the field for over a year. The condition had developed just as Will was storming the world rugby scene, and I was keen to hear what tools he had used to deal with having to put his dreams on hold to deal with a medical condition around which there seemed to be very little certainty, as well as the challenges he'd faced when we were at school.

'I reckon the biggest challenge for a teenager in that resilience space is what motivates them — internal versus external motivation,' Will told me. 'I look back to where I was at when I was at school. Your peers' opinions, team selection, grades, popularity . . . all that sort of stuff is what's driving you. Whereas I think, reflecting on the last few years I've had in professional sport, what I've found sustainable is more around having internal motivators to guide me. That makes it a lot easier to overcome those worries.'

Will gave an example from early in his career with the Crusaders that sums this up pretty well. And don't think this is just a rugby story — its lesson is applicable to life in general.

'When I first came into the Crusaders, we had a really strong team with Dave Havili at fullback [Will's preferred position], and so I'd play one game, then get dropped the next week. It played on my mind a lot, and I found myself always trying to play a lot like David, trying to emulate his style. Because of that, when coaches would give me feedback, I took it really personally — it was like "this guy's better than you", because I was trying to *be* him and wasn't achieving it.

'When I started to get a few more games together, I began to realise it was actually more important for me to just go out there and play *my* game. Trying to copy someone else's game was just not helpful. Once I understood that, getting the feedback felt less like criticism and more like a growth opportunity.

'That, for me, was the switch from external to internal motivation — from wanting to be better to impress the coaches, to instead wanting to have any feedback around what I was doing to try to grow myself. That was the start of a change from me from playing okay but inconsistently, to playing a lot better, but also just feeling a lot happier — a lot more excited to rock up, a lot less worried about making mistakes — because I was comfortable with how I operated and who I was as a player.

'When you're in the bubble of a school, it's hard to see beyond that. But I think it starts with finding stuff that genuinely interests you and not basing your self-esteem off other people's opinions.'

One of the things I really wanted to understand was how Will copes with the pressure, and the highs and lows which come with being a professional player in a rugby-mad country — one week you can be the match-winning hero, and the next week you can be a failure and a national pariah. How could you live with that, let alone go out and perform to a high level under the weight of all that expectation and responsibility?

Will's response struck me as something which we can all relate to. He said one of the keys is to try not to 'ride the wave', being buoyed up and then dragged down by other people's opinions.

'In rugby, if you have a good game, you go on Instagram and heaps of people are hyping you up, like "This guy's a legend". That's fine, but if you get a real kick from that, then when the negative things come, when you have a bad game and you read the comments, then you also get a massive drop — so you end up with huge fluctuations. If you just don't engage with any of that external stuff, you don't have to ride that wave.

'I've always been a big believer in celebrating your successes — when you do things well, it's important to be able to acknowledge that, and then reset. But it's not about reading comments to pump up your tyres.'

At school, Will always seemed like a pretty formidable force — he was as talented academically as he was good at sport. So I was interested to hear him say that it didn't feel like a smooth ride to him at the time.

'I was born late for my year group, February, so I was always one of the youngest, and a little bit less mature than a few others in terms of life experiences like drinking, girls and social stuff, so that was where I struggled in terms of finding my place. Years 9 and 10 were the time I struggled the most with trying to find where I was going to fit in. Physically, I hadn't grown yet, so I was quite small and short' — Will pauses here and courteously notes that there's nothing wrong with that — 'and that physical side played with my head on the social side.'

Funnily enough, I do recall this, because in year 10 I was taller than Will. The reason I remember this, more than ten years on, is that I was also pretty short, and at the time I shared the same insecurity about my height. I used to be very aware of the height of other people in my class. The irony is that Will now towers over me, at 188 cm (6 foot 2 inches), whereas I've barely got any taller at all since year 10 — perhaps why Will insists that 'there's nothing wrong with being short'!

Will continued: 'By the time I got to the end of year 12, I was in a much better space, but I'd been through a few tough nights of stressing about it, for sure. I'd made the First XV and the First XI, and you just sort of find like-minded mates through sport like that. I think time fixes a few of those worries for you.'

I asked Will if he had any advice he would give himself, if he could talk to his younger self:

'Just be open to new stuff and giving things a go. The more opportunities you take, the more chances you give yourself to find that purpose, and to work out what you don't want, which I think is just as important. Just take opportunities.'

# 4

# SALVAGE

**salvage (verb):** to rescue or save, especially from wreckage or ruin; to succeed in achieving something in a situation or action that has been a failure.

When my cancer was first diagnosed, there was discussion about putting me on a type of treatment known as 'salvage protocol'. Now I'm no doctor, but when the actual doctors start talking about trying to 'salvage' you, it's a fair bet that you're in a pretty sticky situation.

The first part of the definition above is actually quite important. To salvage something does not mean to prevent or avert the initial wreckage or ruin — that part still happens. The act of salvaging is being able to get something out of or save something from the situation. The doctors couldn't undo the fact I had cancer, but they could try to get the best possible outcome out of it: keeping me alive.

Now that I've fully recovered from both my cancer and the treatment, the idea of always trying to salvage something good from the bad has become a core pillar of my approach to resilience in the face of all forms of adversity. It helped me hugely going through chemo, and has remained ingrained in me since my time in hospital.

Most of the time, life is fairly predictable — not in terms of exactly what will happen, but in terms of the mix of good and bad things. Some interesting research a while back showed that all of the people in this study generally experienced the same amount of positive and negative events in each day, but the people who were better at recognising the positive events were far happier.

You can divide everything which happens in a given day into one of four categories:

1. Big wins (uncommon)
2. Small wins (frequent)
3. Big losses (uncommon)
4. Small losses (frequent).

Number 1s and 3s don't come along that often. Most of our days are made up of a combination of number 2- and 4-type events, in roughly equal quantities.

There are exceptions to this rule, however. One odd thing about life is that you seem to occasionally hit hot streaks and cold streaks. Sometimes you'll have a week, or month, or year, where things just seem to go your way. The cards all fall in your favour, you tick off goal after goal. Things which could've gone wrong just don't. You're on fire!

Then other times, you seem to hit roadblock after roadblock. They say bad things come in threes, but sometimes it's like they come in thirties. You know it's one of those days, weeks, months, when something else goes wrong and your first reaction is just to start laughing in disbelief. Perhaps your perception has been shaped by what has already happened — but we all know the feeling of being on one of those streaks of good or bad. Fortunately, most of the time it's a balance, a give-and-take, a win-some lose-some . . . a bit of both.

Part of the unfair nature of life is that when you have a big win, it can easily be ruined by a big loss — picking up some excellence credits or making the team you trialled for just isn't going to shine all that bright if your dog gets hit by a car the next day. But worse yet, it's not even a fair trade-off, because it doesn't go the other way: if your dog gets hit by a car, getting a few credits or making the team the next day isn't going to make it any better. Big losses can ruin big wins, but big wins can't fix big losses — unfair, right?

In fact, often big losses or great adversity can completely prevent you from getting big wins. When I was in hospital, I didn't have a pathway to make the team, nor could I get out of bed to go to my exams — although maybe that was a small win in itself.

Adversity, particularly significant adversity, has a way of stifling potential joy, success and happiness. It also robs us of the small wins we previously may have relied on, because it disrupts the patterns and schedules we have built our lives around, the things which typically bring us joy. Often without us even realising, all of the things which used to bring us positive emotion are taken away from us by the circumstances we find ourselves in. In hospital, I didn't get to grab lunch with mates, or head out to a party on the weekend. All the little wins were gone.

It's in those times that the unfortunate reality is that you are left with nothing more than what you choose to deliberately look for. No big wins are coming your way, and none of the regular small wins you used to rely on are there anymore, helping to get you through. If you want anything to make you happy, you'd better be ready to go out and find it for yourself. That's where the idea of Salvaging comes in.

There are two aspects to it, which I'll discuss below. Both are critical tools to being resilient in the face of adversity, and finding a way through bad things to survive and thrive on the other side.

## Finding the Good Within the Bad

Some people call it looking for the silver lining of the cloud. Others talk about finding the light within the darkness. Whatever you call it, in the early stages of my cancer treatment, it became pretty clear to me that there weren't many upsides, apart from the fact that it would probably save my life. Aside from that, there weren't going to be many big wins along the way; in fact, there weren't a heap of small wins either. So I realised pretty early on that I needed to get creative in how I found anything good at all amongst this backdrop of bad — because, unfortunately, that was all I had left.

I consciously made an effort to do this. Whenever I was faced with a new challenge or form of adversity, my head would jump straight to trying to scramble and rearrange it into something which could be considered even slightly positive.

Here are a few examples. On a particularly rough day, I might think, 'Yes, I've got my head in a bucket right now — but I'll probably never, ever feel as sick as I do now again in my entire life. This is the sickest I will ever feel, and that's pretty sweet.' Or, 'Yes, I can't go out and live a normal life like all of my mates are right now — but some of them are coming to visit me later today, and that's fantastic.' Or, 'Yes, I've got to have a gruesome and agonising spinal injection of chemo today — but it means I'll be bed-bound for the rest of the afternoon, so I don't have to get up and do physio exercises, because boy do I hate being made to walk circles around a chair in my room.'

> I made a conscious choice to try to feed whatever information I had coming in through the lens of 'what in this is a positive?' — and surprisingly, more often than not, I found something.

There's one story which possibly captures this better than any other.

In hospital, as you may or may not know, you order your food by ticking little boxes on a piece of paper, which gets collected and taken away the day before. Let's not get into talking about hospital food — they do a pretty admirable job of trying to feed a whole lot of people — all you need to know is that for breakfast every day, I picked toast. You also got to choose spreads. I chose butter (because having cancer was suffering enough, I didn't need margarine to top it off), Marmite and jam. No option to specify the type of jam, which got my attention because while I'm far from a fussy eater, there's no one who can tell me that strawberry jam is better than raspberry jam.

Early in my stay, during those first fifty-two days I was confined, I hit a cold streak. Morning after morning, day after day, it was strawberry jam after strawberry jam. Each morning I would scramble to the cupboard through the wall into which my food had been put (because as few people as possible were allowed into the room because of my immunocompromised state) and check the jam label. Each day started the same way — with sickly sweet disappointment.

Of course, I could have resolved this pretty easily, by writing 'raspberry please!' on the food menu sheet, or by asking my parents to bring me a stash of my own raspberry jam. That wasn't the point, though. Each morning I rushed to check the cupboard because I knew that the wait for some raspberry jam would be worth it, and each day that it wasn't there, I knew the greater my excitement would be when it was.

Picture the scene . . . I'm truly visually distressing, about 15 kilograms lighter than I should be, missing my eyebrows and eyelashes, and completely bald on top. I look like someone dying of cancer. I'm locked in an isolation room, in the basement of the hospital, next to the morgue, surrounded by people just as sick as me. And one morning, as I get my cold toast out of the cupboard in the wall, I find I have been given . . . raspberry jam.

Then picture this sick young guy literally fist-pumping the air, jumping up and down as much as my wasted leg muscles would allow, in absolute joy. I don't think I'll ever find a breakfast which will beat that morning's one.

It's a ridiculous story really, even an embarrassing one. You might think I'm completely insane, or that I need to get out more. But I've never forgotten that moment, and whenever I'm in a tricky situation where I doubt there's any good to be found within it, when all seems hopeless, I remember me on chemo, in a place surrounded by death and despair, and how much joy one little sachet of raspberry jam can bring.

This attitude of deliberately seeking out the good, the positive in any situation really is a skill — something I learnt and had plenty of time to practise in hospital — and hopefully I'll keep it for life, because it has continued to have a powerful impact on my ability to get through tough times since then: my ability to be resilient. As with the concept of Slowing Down discussed in the previous chapter, research shows that people who can look for the good in the bad have better outcomes than people who do not. In psychology, this is known as realistic optimism, which we'll get on to in more detail shortly — but it's one of the key indicators of how well someone is able to get through adversity, and it's something which you can learn to do.

Start by capturing the obvious silver linings, and then apply the same logic to bigger problems where the benefits are harder to find. It's an amazing thing to be able to do — offsetting or minimising some of the pain and sadness which comes from adversity by finding something good within it. This is the philosophy of

Salvaging on a micro level: trying to find any little bit of good at each and every moment during that adversity, to keep your spirits high and encourage yourself to keep moving forward.

There's a second part to the philosophy of Salvaging, and that's salvaging on a big scale — trying to find not just the *small* good things within the bad (like raspberry jam in hospital), but the *big* good things as well (like the opportunity to try to help people because of my cancer). Taking it a step further, it's finding ways in which *the bad things themselves* can be made into good things.

In a sense, my whole approach to cancer has been a form of this in action — trying to find the good within the bad. Trying to salvage something from the adversity. Taking the challenge of cancer and turning it into an opportunity to try to help other people. Turning something bad into something good by looking for the possibilities within it.

I'm not the only one who thinks this way — Paralympian Liam Malone, whose interview follows this chapter, has encountered some really tough times in his life, including losing his mum at a young age:

> 'I had a fantastic mum, and I was very dependent on her growing up. So, one way that I look at her death, and maybe it sounds like a terrible way to look at it, is like perhaps I wouldn't have developed the level of responsibility that I have for owning my actions unless she'd passed away.'

Liam has also been able to get his head around losing his legs as a young child by appreciating all the good that has come about because of this undoubtedly difficult event.

> 'I feel very lucky to be the person that ended up having no legs. You know, maybe someone else wouldn't have enjoyed the journey as much as I have. So I don't think I'd change anything about my situation. It's been pretty enjoyable.'

........

I know there will be some people out there thinking, 'It's easy for him to say, "Look what good came out of my adversity", but *my* adversity doesn't feel like it has a silver lining, nor anything I can salvage from it right now.' To that person, you're not wrong, and it *is* easy for me to say that in my fortunate position. There is good news, though. While you might not be able to see it right now, there is always something good which can be found in adversity, and the greater the adversity and suffering, the greater the opportunity to salvage it. We just have to look at the bigger picture.

One of the most well-documented forms of positive change salvaged from adversity is something called post-traumatic growth. That's not to be confused with post-traumatic stress disorder or PTSD, which is the opposite but equally possible outcome of a traumatic life event or significant adversity. Post-traumatic growth or PTG is, as the name suggests, *personal growth and development which occurs because of adversity*. It's what happens when we create something good out of something shit, and make purpose out of suffering — ensuring that the bad times weren't all for nothing. To *salvage* something. And it's applicable regardless of whether we're talking about cancer, or a loved one dying, or a broken toe the week before tournament week.

Psychologists reckon that, after a person faces adversity or a challenge in life, there are three possible outcomes: survive, recover or thrive.

- To *survive* is to get through the event but be left permanently negatively affected on the whole — to never fully recover from what happened.
- To *recover* is to get back to the baseline you were at before the traumatic event. You're no better or worse than before, just the same.
- To *thrive*, however, is to *be left better than before by the challenge which you faced; to be improved by the adversity; changed in a positive way.*

As improbable as this may sound, this outcome is very possible, and certainly how I would define my experience with cancer.

So what changes are brought about by post-traumatic growth? What actually gets altered about you? The changes which make up post-traumatic growth are often anchored in core pillars of your life, such as relationships, self-beliefs and life philosophies — and for that reason, they're often significant and noticeable. When people ask me what I think cancer has changed about me, the answer they get is always the same: 'It would be quicker for me to list the things cancer *hasn't* changed.' And that's not just some cheesy line.

The key things which psychologists say characterise post-traumatic growth are, in my own words:

1. Heightened sense of gratitude
2. Improved relationships
3. Increased resilience and emotional strength
4. Finding greater purpose
5. New opportunities.

So, how does my experience of post-traumatic growth after my cancer measure up?

*Heightened sense of gratitude*: big tick. If you've been paying attention, you'll be well aware by now that this is one of the most significant factors of my life which came from my adversity.

Initially, I experienced overwhelming, nauseating, exhausting gratitude. Gratitude for everything. I remember a phase, just after my legs had begun to recover from the nerve damage, where I was immeasurably grateful for the ability to use my legs again. To be able to roll over in bed at night. To stand unsupported without fear of keeling over and hitting the deck. That was a hectic few months, with each and every single step bringing a ping of gratitude. Even after the first few months of unrestrained gratitude about everything settled down, I still feel so much more gratitude about every aspect of my life than I did before cancer.

*Improved relationships*: tick. Cancer brought me closer to the people in my life than anything else (bar some other significant adversity) ever could have. It was one of the greatest wins out of what I went through. The trust and connection I built and strengthened with them over this time is unmatched. There's a simple reason for this: vulnerability creates trust, and trust creates connection. Cancer created plenty of vulnerability — like when I lost my eyebrows and eyelashes and every bloody hair on my body, when I was completely dependent and had to rely on the people around me for everything I needed. The upside of that was how it strengthened my relationships and sense of connection with those around me.

*Increased resilience and emotional strength*: big tick. Well, you're holding a book I've written about it, so you'd sure hope I'd experienced this change! Fortunately, I can say for a fact that I am more resilient thanks to my cancer, because as I've been saying, adversity provides the opportunity to train and hone your resilience. That is often the greatest form of meaning that you can find in challenging situations — the chance to learn from them and prepare yourself for the future. And typically, the greater the adversity, the greater the resilience you can gain. Adversity also often teaches us that we *already have* so much more resilience than we thought, tucked up our sleeve somewhere. Finding it in our moment of need is pretty empowering.

*Finding greater purpose*: tick. Often, adversity is something we have to go through to find out what we really want from our lives. I know more than a few cancer nurses who took that path because they'd had cancer themselves, or a sibling or parent had experienced it. I came to realise through my own journey that I want to help other people face their own adversity. This wasn't a focus for me before cancer — now, it's what I care about most of all. I know that without cancer my head would probably be in a very different place.

Another big positive which came out of the resilience I gained is that I'm a far more optimistic, glass half-full kind of person than I was before the cancer — not in a cheesy, 'she'll be right', weirdly happy way, but in a factual, 'I have overcome something worse than this and therefore I am capable of creating a plan to get through any adversity' kind of way. *Resilience is the basis for my optimism.* I know now that I can get through so much more because of what I have learnt about how to overcome tough times.

That is another positive outcome of facing adversity, and a form of meaning to find in suffering: *the chance to prove to yourself just how capable you are, thereby gaining the confidence to go forward in life feeling that you can overcome challenges when you inevitably need to, and hence feeling a little more optimistic for the future.* In psychology, this is known as self-efficacy — your belief in your own ability to do something. In this case, being resilient.

*New opportunities*: Well hey, I certainly wouldn't be writing this right now if it wasn't for my cancer. Nor would I have had any of the other opportunities it has given me. Can't really complain about that!

Experiencing these five changes — a heightened sense of gratitude, improved relationships, increased resilience and emotional strength, finding greater purpose and being given new opportunities — have in turn led to a level of satisfaction in my life that I don't think I could have imagined before, or without, my cancer.

It's hard to believe I owe that all to cancer, or adversity, or bad times in general — but that is the reality. This is why I tell people that, if I had my time over again, I'd still choose to have had the cancer, because of what it has taught me, and the meaning I was able to find in suffering. This is post-traumatic growth, and it can come from any adversity you have to face in your life, regardless of how big it is.

I can't tell you what impact post-traumatic growth might have on you. Nor can I tell you about the impact of any past adversity that you have overcome. Only you can look at yourself, and perhaps with the help of those around you, measure the changes that have occurred within you.

.........

So that all sounds great, right? That even if you do encounter significant adversity, there's still a chance to get something really positive out of it? I do have to say, though, this kind of post-traumatic growth won't just drop into your lap. You have to make a concerted effort to create and take positives away from adversity and suffering. Post-traumatic growth is *not* guaranteed, but you can give yourself the best possible odds of achieving it.

Psychologists have researched what sets apart people who thrive after adversity from people who only survive or recover. Part of it relates to the attitude that you take into the adversity — a conscious awareness of the fact that some good can come from it. Well, good news — now you are aware! More specifically — and this is important — you now understand that good can come from *you and your response* to the adversity. I'm not suggesting that loss, or pain, or suffering, or failure is a good thing, nor is it something you'd ever choose.

> But within yourself, you have the ability to create something positive from something undeniably traumatic. In doing so, you reduce the pain of the adversity. You can create meaning, or purpose, or a positive outcome, which can to some degree offset the negative outcomes or emotions of the experience.

The attitude that you take into adversity has been proven to significantly impact how well a person copes or deals with the adversity, and the long-term outcomes. Luckily for us, psychologists have made a list of the most useful attitude traits. They are:

1. Realistic (or honest) optimism
2. Feeling in control
3. Positive coping style
4. Sense of self.

Let's break those down and explain them a little further. Firstly, what do they mean by *realistic optimism*? As I said before, we're not talking about the mindless, head-in-space, everything-is-going-to-be-great kind of optimism. It's about being able to face challenges with a *realistic appraisal of both the good and the bad in a situation, with a willingness to find the good.*

Often in times of struggle, it can be easy to turn off the 'good' tap and just languish under the stream of misery and pity. It becomes a cycle, where negative experiences and emotions set you up to find more and more negatives. Maintaining some honest optimism is not about lying to yourself or hiding from the challenge of a situation. It is about acknowledging and accepting that it might be bad — but also equally accepting that it might not be *all* bad.

The second aspect, *feeling in control*, also very much relates to what I talked about before, in terms of what gives me the ability to feel optimistic. *At the core of what makes any experience traumatic is the lack of control you feel you have over it.* If it were controllable, it would be avoidable — you could prevent failure, death, loss. If a situation is somewhat controllable, it is more manageable. The more control you feel you have over adversity, the less daunting it becomes.

'How on Earth would that work?' you ask. 'You literally just said all of the worst adversity is out of my control!'

But when psychologists talk about control, they aren't talking about controlling the situation in terms of what actually happens, but rather *your response to and interaction with it.* They are talking about how you can take active steps to try to deal with your experience in a positive way — for instance, reaching out for help, or investing time and effort into taking care of yourself instead of allowing all parts of your life to fall apart just because one area is being challenged. *It's about doing your best, putting in an effort, and therefore knowing you're exerting some control over your situation and the adversity.* You're fighting back, not just letting it crush you.

There is also much to be said for the *expectation of adversity*: an understanding that things are going to go terribly wrong sometimes, and that this is unavoidable. This isn't a reason, nor an excuse, to be pessimistic or live in fear of the worst. Rather, it's the ability to understand that adversity is part of life, and *you will make it through*. As gloomy and daunting as that sounds, this is an important step towards increasing your resilience, because if we have an inbuilt expectation of adversity, when tough times come along, it's more 'Well, here we are, what do we do now?' as opposed to 'Why me? Why did this have to happen? This is awful.' In essence, *you meet adversity with the attitude of a survivor rather than a victim*. And that will bolster your feeling of control over that situation.

Thirdly, you will do better if your *coping style* is a positive one. People tend to cope with adversity in one of two ways: being active or avoidant. As the name suggests, being avoidant means your actions or thoughts are focused towards denying, minimising, and yes, avoiding dealing with the adversity and, more specifically, the emotions it brings up. Some ways of avoiding facing adversity include drinking or drugs, isolating yourself or withdrawing socially, sleeping too much, denying there is a problem, or generally not engaging with the issue because it makes you feel bad. Sometimes this is also called escapism. Unfortunately, this coping style isn't actually 'coping' at all, and doesn't lead to a resolution or solving the problem.

Active coping, on the other hand, is also pretty much what the name suggests: having intent and taking action to engage with the adversity and the emotions surrounding it. It's not running away or trying to hide from your problems, nor the feelings which arise from these problems. Here's a list of some active coping strategies, which (not coincidentally) covers a lot of what we're talking about in this book:

- seeking support
- problem-solving
- physical activity
- self-care
- using humour.

Humour in particular is a key predictor of post-traumatic growth and increased resilience — and we'll come to that shortly.

Finally, your *sense of self*. Sense of self is quite a deep and varied concept in the world of psychology, but it's considered to be a critical part of living a successful and happy life. In short, your sense of self is effectively your ability to comprehend your 'life narrative' and who you are. It is a sense of self-awareness, recognising your strengths and weaknesses, understanding what has happened to you in your life and why, how it relates to you, and what impact that has on your actions and reactions. It is having good self-esteem and backing yourself. In practice, it is the ability to make sense of the things which go wrong for you, and understand how you can best navigate through them by drawing on your strengths and minimising your weaknesses.

If there was some kind of physical comparison to draw to a strong mental sense of self, it would be those gymnasts who can do those tumbling/flipping/twisting things where they run and then spring across the mat in a blur of energy. That awareness of self and their position in space, knowing intuitively the actions they need to take next to keep this masterful move going (rather than breaking their neck), and the confidence they must have to commit to the manoeuvre, is the physical embodiment of having a strong sense of self. Sounds cooler now, right?

So how do you get some of this? Well, in large part, it comes from having *purpose and meaning* in your life (and we'll talk more about that in chapter 8). Having a sense of meaning enables you to have self-belief and understanding. It boosts self-esteem, and it gives you something larger to which your overall existence can be tied. What this allows, in practice, is *transcendence: being able to make sense of adversity as part of the larger picture of progress, or life, or achievement of a goal or purpose.* This is really, really powerful stuff, and not half as airy-fairy as it sounds.

These four aspects — honest optimism, feeling in control, positive coping style, and sense of self — contribute towards an overall attitude which will set you up to experience something good out of adversity: that post-traumatic growth. It's not a guarantee that things will be easy, nor is it any form of escape or respite from the adversity, but it's your best option for salvaging something good from something bad, on a big level. And your ability to do this, to salvage, will make you more resilient.

## Finding Humour in Tough Times

When I was first diagnosed with my cancer, after that week of gruesome medical procedures and tests, my family and I were given the news together. Shortly afterwards, they were sent out of the room so that my doctor could discuss my treatment with me privately, as I was eighteen years and three months old, and so technically an adult with a right to decide my own care without my parents being part of the conversation. After my family left the room I had a fairly serious chat with my haematologist. The core of this chat centred around some key things:

1. You've got the fastest-growing cancer known to man.
2. Without treatment, you've got about two weeks to live.
3. Even if you have treatment, you better keep your fingers and toes crossed that you survive.
4. Oh, and if you do survive the treatment, your balls might not work anymore — you could be left infertile. So, if you think you want to have kids, ever (please decide this right now, while you're eighteen and have just been informed of the three prior points), we will need to put some needles in your testicles. Tomorrow. And by some, we mean four.

Superb, great chat.

My family shuffled back into the room, shoulders down and faces pointed at the ground, crying in unison, like they were already taking part in a funeral procession. Naturally, I felt pretty compelled to offer some poignant words.

I turned to my uncle.

*Me: Pick a star sign beginning with C.*

My uncle (between poorly disguised sniffs and wipes of eyes): Uh . . . Capricorn?

*Me: The doctor says I've got the other one.*

This was simultaneously the best and worst joke I have ever made. It's certainly the best example of timing, and the worst example of playing to an audience. If you didn't find that funny, I hope that's because it's a terrible joke, not because you feel it would be wrong to laugh about it, because it's not — I mean, I'd only had the right to make cancer jokes for about 90 seconds and I was already cracking into them.

My family were not the only unfortunate people on the receiving end of my attempts at humour during the dark and trying times that followed. My friends, who I already knew were great value, continued to provide the same banter which I'd always enjoyed, from the messages they wrote on the whiteboard on my hospital-room wall ('unluggy uce', 'sucks to be you'), through to the text messages they sent me as I lay in my room ('you still alive over there?'), to the comebacks they gave when I tried to pipe up and defend myself ('that's a lot of chat coming from a bloke with no eyebrows').

There's one infamous story which I have shared with audiences many times in response to a question I often receive during Q&As: what can I do and say to support my friend who is going through cancer?

Early in my treatment, when I was still far from being out of the woods, a friend sent me this poem:

Hold On, Pain Ends.

Ignore The Sorrows, The Errors, Regrets Made.
Inspire Nations, Appreciate Life.

It's a pretty decent poem, particularly considering it was written by an eighteen-year-old bloke for his eighteen-year-old friend who has just been diagnosed with cancer. As I sat there in my hospital bed reading it — a little bit perplexed why one of my mates was being so soppy, but accepting that people respond in all kinds of ways to bad news — he sent me a follow-up text: 'It's an acrostic poem, read the first letter of each word.' A few of the doctors and nurses looked confused when they saw the words 'HOPE IT'S TERMINAL' written across my whiteboard the next day.

I tell this story a lot because it perfectly illustrates my answer to the question 'What can I do to support my friend?' . . . because, for me, the answer is to treat them exactly as you did before they were diagnosed. As young guys, we used to relentlessly banter and joke and give each other shit, from a place of love — and for me, it was incredibly important that my diagnosis did not mean the end of this humour and laughter, because this was the time when I would need it most. I knew they were all there for me, including if I actually wanted to talk about how it was really going or what I was feeling — but in the meantime, humour kept things light.

No doubt you've experienced this as well — laughing at inappropriate moments or situations, or making jokes out of things you probably wouldn't have imagined yourself being able to joke about. Sometimes bad times are funny, but why? Why would I be cracking jokes minutes after finding out I might only have two weeks left to live? How could my mind even let me do that?

The answer is simple: laughter is good for you. It has a bunch of positive impacts on the body — physiological changes that occur when you laugh, which make you feel better. Just like when you exercise, when you laugh your body releases feel-good chemicals such as endorphins and dopamine. It increases your heart rate, blood pressure, circulation, immune-system activity and alertness, then after you stop laughing, your blood pressure, heart rate, muscle activity and rate of breathing temporarily reduce, resulting in a sense of relaxation.

> Put simply, the act of laughter puts physical processes into play which reduce emotional pain and calm you. Because of this, your brain is desperate to find humour and create laughter in those moments when you most need this relief.

You can see it in outbursts of nervous laughter, which is your body trying to draw on those benefits to help you in stressful situations.

It should be no surprise, then, that studies have shown the ability to use laughter and humour during adversity creates greater emotional wellbeing. The more you can laugh during tough times, the more likely you are to receive these benefits, which include significant decreases in depression, anxiety and stress levels, and significant increases in self-belief, positive emotions, optimism and feelings of control. This is why laughter is a natural coping mechanism.

Looking back on my own time in hospital, I saw this in action with the nurses who were taking care of me: people with the most razor-sharp, at times dark, but always hilarious senses of humour I'd ever met. Why? Because they spend their days cleaning up a variety of human bodily fluids, working insane hours, and watching patients who they have become close to suffer and sometimes die — day after day, year after year.

Consequently, they have to adapt to survive this harsh and brutal reality, and they do this in part by laughing — a lot. Because honestly, what's the alternative? If they cried every time something went wrong, they would cry all day, every day — so they laugh instead. Of all the things I love and respect about nurses, it is their resilience which I respect most of all, and their sense of humour plays a big part in this.

••••••••

There's more to this than physical effects, though. There's something psychologically very powerful about being able to laugh at adversity — as though if you're laughing, then it really can't be that bad. If you're laughing, you're still hanging in there. And, as we'll go on to discuss in chapter 8, *to be able to laugh in the face of adversity diminishes some of its power and control over you*. I've found that myself many times.

During the cancer, despite the adversity I was facing I would actively try to be optimistic and keep laughing. If I was laughing,

I felt as if I was exerting my power over my situation, rather than letting it exert *its* power over *me* by stopping me from being happy. So, often during my treatment, and particularly when times were toughest, I would make a deliberate effort to find the humour in a situation. Take point 4 at the start of this section — the whole needles-in-balls thing.

Maybe that doesn't sound funny to you. Maybe, and particularly if you also have testicles, you might be wondering how laughing about this would make it any better. But look at the alternative — what would have happened if I hadn't joked about it? I would've laid in bed, feeling sore and squeamish, ashamed and embarrassed to share it with people, and certainly feeling super-awkward every few hours as a male nurse came into my room to check on me and, as I lay there in silence, literally cupped my junk in his hand to check on the swelling. I could have very easily holed up in my hospital room and sat silently by myself ruminating on the terrible situation — and I don't think anyone would have thought that was an inappropriate reaction.

But would I have felt any better? Would it have given me hope or confidence, or made it feel any easier? Would it have eased my emotions? Instead, sitting in my hospital bed with the nurses and family and friends I had around me, I had some genuine, hearty laughs about what was going on. This disarmed the whole situation, and took the horror and embarrassment out of it for everybody. If I could laugh about it, so could my friends. This laughter drew us closer together, strengthened our bonds, and gave me physical and emotional relief when I needed it most.

*Choosing to laugh was one of those pivotal moments in my cancer, when it could've gone one way or the other*. Had I chosen to shut down that opportunity to make things feel a little lighter, then I would've been sitting there feeling seriously sorry for myself. Choosing to laugh lessened that burden. It shrank the adversity to be smaller than me, so it couldn't overwhelm me anymore. If I could laugh in its face then it did not control me.

It also allowed the people around me to help carry me forward. That shared humour drew them close to me, to share in my experiences and to be there for me to lean on. And I have no doubt that it made my family and the people who cared about me feel more at ease as well, because they saw that I was doing okay, which gave them one less thing to worry about in the moment.

I guess you could say that all these jokes were at my expense — after all, I'm the one who had cancer. But I think that's a really important part of Laughing Through The Tough Times and, in a wider sense, resilience — you have to be able to laugh at yourself, to make jokes at your own expense, because otherwise you won't be able to laugh at all. If you're not willing to cop a bit of humour on the chin, whether it's mates giving you some friendly stick or having a laugh about a nurse checking your balls, then you're going to have a very tough time finding the humour and getting all these benefits which come from it — the physiological effects, the closeness and connection to others, the ability to push back against adversity and feel the power and control which comes from that — because there's not much else you're going to find yourself laughing about. During times of adversity you might not be able to laugh about the things you might usually laugh about, but you *are* going to be able to laugh about the things you usually wouldn't.

........

That's all very well, you might be thinking, but how am I supposed to laugh? In the face of adversity, of suffering, how can I possibly find humour?

You'll find it. Trust me, if you look for it, you'll find it. Throughout my treatment, I didn't know what was going to be thrown my way, but when it happened, we took the opportunity to laugh. Whenever you find yourself in adversity, you can find a way to make fun of it. There are a few things you can do which might help you see the lighter side:

1. *Approach situations of adversity from the perspective that they might be funny*. Be open to the *idea* that it could be funny — which is often where people who don't laugh through adversity go wrong. If you're firmly of the opinion that what is happening is a disaster, a catastrophe, and nothing will make it better, then you're 100 per cent correct on all counts. On the other hand, if you're open to finding the humour in these times, then it'll be there. If you think things that are 'not funny' in traditional terms (e.g. cancer) might be funny, then you open yourself up to the opportunity to laugh about them. If you just view things that are unfunny as being unfunny,

then they will remain unfunny. (This is what happens when your dad makes dad jokes.)

2. *Move the timeframe*. This is an easy one to grasp. Things are often funnier in retrospect, right? We all have memories of times where we were angry or scared or sad, but looking back on them now, we can laugh about what happened. After the moment has passed, and the negative emotion attached to that moment has faded a bit, you can more easily see what was funny, rather than being fixated on what was sad or scary or embarrassing. Instead of waiting for this to happen, however, try to see this 'retrospective' view in the present moment. Shift yourself mentally into the future, and ask yourself what you might find funny about this moment *with the benefit of time*. Often, that'll make it easier to see the humour.
3. *Try to see the situation from an external perspective*. Imagine one of your friends seeing the situation, for example. This is one of the great benefits of friends: they can change the way you view a situation. Throughout my cancer treatment, I knew there would be plenty my mates would be laughing about. To be clear, my mates weren't laughing at my cancer, or at me for having cancer, but there were plenty of situations or moments stemming from that adversity which I knew would crack them up — like when my accounting teacher theorised aloud to the class that I was pulling a prolonged sickie to get out of school, about twenty-four hours before he found

> out I had cancer. I got a good laugh out of that — as did the rest of the class when they saw his face when he found out! In my darkest moments in hospital, I would try to picture myself sitting around in someone's lounge retelling this story, sharing a few laughs with my mates about what happened, and imagining what their reaction would be. Doing this gave me that critical bit of distance between myself and my suffering. It allowed me the clarity of mind to be able to see the good, the light, the funny in a moment when I was struggling to see beyond the emotions I was feeling at that time.

Applying these three little tweaks to your thinking, as minor as they sound, can make a world of difference.

I was *not* open to the idea of losing my eyebrows during chemotherapy treatment being funny at first, because goddamn was it alarming. Literally, I looked alarmed. People with no eyebrows look perpetually surprised, like they've raised their eyebrows so high they're now on the back of their head. But when I opened my mind to it maybe, possibly, being *a bit* funny; then when I moved the timeframe and viewed it from the perspective of how I would feel about it in the future once they'd grown back; then finally when I thought about how my friends would feel about it, how they would react, and what they would say (there were a hell of a lot of jokes and laughter at my expense) . . . I finally managed to see the lighter side of my lack of eyebrows. The negative way I viewed it, and the emotions of shame and sadness that I felt, were diminished.

It doesn't have to be something as serious as losing your eyebrows to cancer, though. Calling your teacher 'Mum' by mistake (I think I have every single one of the five times I've done this burnt into my brain) might not feel funny in the moment, but god knows it does to all your mates who are howling with laughter. In retrospect, with a bit of time, it will to you as well. The same three principles are in play.

By applying these three strategies, you've got a much better chance of finding something, *anything*, which can allow you to reap the benefits of humour during adversity. After all, that's when you need it most — laughter during the good times is great, but it's a hell of a lot more powerful and beneficial if you're doing it when things aren't going well.

I think this is one of my favourite things about facing adversity — being able to make light of it. After all, that's how you can conquer it most fully. It's one thing to trudge through, to just survive and get out the other side, roughed up and beaten down, and if that's the only way you can get through then you know you've given it your best shot. But if you can get through with a smile on your face, and a laugh with those who are by your side, then you've got through it better, without a doubt.

.........

One more thing: I've been accused once or twice before of hiding from adversity (or being avoidant) because I'm able to laugh about it — as though approaching it with humour means I'm not taking it seriously enough. Perhaps you see it this way too, or are afraid that laughing through the tough times will make it look like you're trying to distract yourself from your problems or divert attention from them.

I see the exact opposite of this: to be able to laugh about adversity, you must first have considered, accepted and embraced it. To laugh about it is not to hide from it, but rather to employ a recognised strategy to overcome it — to ease the intensity of your emotions, draw people close, and remove any power or control that adversity would otherwise hold over you.

That isn't hiding from adversity, or hiding from your emotions, and refusing to face up to reality. Anyone who says it is doesn't understand it. It's the opposite: it's getting down and wrestling with adversity, making it submit to your own desire to be positive, making it your own personal laughing stock. And that is resilience.

## Summary

- If I had a favourite S, I think it would be Salvage. There's something very powerful about being able to face adversity and suffering with the goal of picking it apart and taking only the good out of it. It feels like you're belittling and ridiculing this force which is trying to break you — and instead, you get to celebrate and find good in it.
- Master this skill and you will feel almost unstoppable. If you can go head-to-head with the things in life which

are theoretically supposed to hurt you, and can turn that power around for your benefit, you're onto a winner.

- There is always a silver lining — challenge yourself to find the good within a bad situation. Sometimes the bad thing can even be turned into a good thing, such as me turning my cancer into the opportunity to teach people about resilience.
- There's truth in the saying 'Laughter is the best medicine'. It's good for you — both mentally and physically — so kick your sense of humour into action whenever you can.

## Liam Malone — Seeking Out the Humour in Tough Times

Liam Malone is, he tells me, a normal guy. 'I've always just considered myself — and this is probably going to sound strange — a regular guy,' is his response when I ask him to characterise his achievements.

'I've had some adversity in my life. I was born with a disability called fibular hemimelia, and some people would consider that adversity. I was eighteen when I lost my mum to cancer. But all in all, it's been a roller coaster of a ride.'

That condition, fibular hemimelia, led to Liam having both of his legs amputated when he was eighteen months old. Having both legs amputated led to, after a fairly indirect road to success, Liam becoming one of New Zealand's best-known and most successful para athletes — a two-time Paralympic gold medallist and one-time silver medallist, and the Paralympic record holder for the 100, 200 and 400 metres sprints — only three years after he set himself the goal. He is a Member of the New Zealand Order of Merit (MNZM).

'But as a person, I'm a regular guy.'

I figured that, particularly before he became a record holder and gold medallist, and got some pretty flash letters after his name, people at school may have viewed things a bit less kindly. I asked Liam about something I'd read: that he wore long trousers the whole way through high school to avoid his prosthetics being on display, because he got so much shit for having no legs.

'You know, the bad part about that time came from me not accepting myself, as opposed to people teasing me. I guess that was magnified by the fact that I didn't feel like I was normal or something. But again, everyone teases everyone at high school. Some people deal with it better than other people, and I dealt with it well, in the sense that I was good at teasing other people, and I was still a confident person. But on the inside, I just didn't accept myself, which is why I wore pants the whole time.

'And obviously, I'm just trying to get a girlfriend. It's hard to get a girlfriend at that age without legs, you know.

'At the end of the day you have to accept yourself, that's on you. If you can't learn that, you'll be forever stuck feeling like you don't fit in, unable to go and do the things you want to do. The one thing I wish I knew back then was that other people were going through similar things, and that everything I felt was completely normal and I wasn't going crazy.'

This must have been a huge part of how Liam built his own resilience as a young person, I remarked — and his response laid out some home truths about resilience. 'The way that you develop resilience, I believe, is the same way that you would train for something. You can train and build resilience, and I think that's a better way to do it than being forced into finding resilience when things suddenly go wrong. For me, obviously, growing up with artificial legs, I was forced to develop resilience. When I started snowboarding, for example, I couldn't ride the T-bar at Rainbow ski field up to the top, so I learnt to snowboard by walking up then riding down until I got to a point where I could take the T-bar up. Playing rugby, my leg would fall off all the time when I would try to kick a ball. Intermediate school, during the 100-metre race, my leg fell off at 50 metres in front of like 1200 kids. They all laughed, and it was f**king devastating. I've just had a lot of circumstances where I've faced an extreme amount of embarrassment, I've failed horrendously, but I've just kept pushing on and built resilience through that.'

I asked Liam about how losing his mum at such a young age shaped his resilience. 'Your character is made up of a combination of your genetics and the accumulation of all your experiences throughout life, and that's certainly one point of life where I was shaped. My mum had cancer for six years. She had been cleared of cancer three times, and it was the last time that it came back that it had metastasized all throughout her body and her organs.

'I came home from school when I was seventeen, where I'd been learning about how cells spread, and I read a letter from a specialist that said the cancer had metastasized to a key organ. At that point, reading that letter, I realised that she was going to die.

'One of the key things that I learnt throughout that experience came from how my mum pretty much continued with life as it was, doing the things that she wanted to do. At that time, I wanted to move to Australia, and she was very encouraging for me to go even though she was on her deathbed. That was a big lesson about pursuing things, even in the face of death and great uncertainty and hardship.

'And then there was the whole "watching someone die" thing. I spent six years in and out of hospitals and hospices, surrounded by people with cancer who are undergoing chemotherapy. You do see people who aren't going to make it out the other side, and you see people who have regrets. You do *not* want to die with regrets — that haunts me to this day. I came away thinking, "If I die, am I going to regret that I didn't do it, or will I regret that I did it and I failed?" Most people conclude that they're going to regret not trying something over trying something and failing. So, I'm not afraid to fail.'

After his mum's passing Liam found himself in Perth, working as a courier driver. It was a dead-end situation, surrounded by deadbeat people. Liam became so efficient at getting his work done that he wound up spending hours of his shifts each day just sleeping in his van — or maybe it was less about how efficient he actually was, and more about how efficient he looked in contrast with his heavily drug-affected colleagues. This time and those stories are something which we have a good laugh about, but which he summarises as 'total f**king misery'.

Feeling that he was on a bit of a road to nowhere, Liam moved back to New Zealand ('Sometimes you just have to write it all off — write off the job, the people, Perth, Australia, write off everything and just start again'). Even with the fresh start, Liam's life remained in a shambles as he struggled to deal with the loss of his mum.

'In time, I just got sick of living that way, and I realised, "I've got to turn this shit around, because I'm largely responsible for how my life is at this point." You can have bad things going on, but it comes down to how you react to them — and that is within your control. That day, I decided I wanted to go to the Paralympics in three years' time, and I started training.

'I've had some success as a result of turning things around, and I've had plenty of failures as well since then — but at least they're all sort of in a positive direction now.'

In the time I've spent with him both during and since this chat, it was pretty clear that Liam has a cracking sense of humour — particularly when it comes to laughing about shit times. I noticed this because, for me, laughing through the tough times is a big part of my own resilience — and it's reassuring to come across someone who makes jokes about having no legs in the same way I joke about having cancer. Liam even did a bit of stand-up comedy after his retirement from running.

'Yeah, for sure. I think humour was the biggest thing, certainly when my mum was sick, and then having no legs and just being the face of embarrassment every Saturday on a rugby field or every day at school — you laugh. You're left with nothing else to do but laugh. There's nothing else that you can do. My leg falls off in front of 1200 kids, and I put my leg back on and I cried and ran to the end, but at the end of the day, all you can do is laugh. You just make fun out of it. The reality is that a lot of life is going to happen to you, and you're not going to be able to control how bad some things will get. If you try to have a laugh as much as possible, and if you can do that in the most dire situations, then you've won.'

As well as that humour, I asked Liam where his resilience has come from throughout his story — from losing his legs, to losing his mum, to his triumphs as a sprinter and now in his successful career since. He was pretty quick to correct me when I characterised losing his legs as adversity, and that in itself felt like an insight into his mindset: 'I feel really lucky to be the person that ended up having no legs. Maybe someone else wouldn't have enjoyed the journey as much as I have.

'Adversity doesn't define you — but your reaction to that adversity certainly does. My story is the most basic example of that — the loss of my legs isn't my identity, but what I did with that has been to some degree.

'You have to do things where you're going to fail. I don't see how you can become resilient without facing the scrutiny of failure. The scrutiny of competition, of putting your ideas out there, of doing things.

'If you're going to become resilient, it's as the by-product of a *forced* situation like going through cancer or having a disability, or as a *voluntary* outcome of pursuing something that is really challenging.

'But it doesn't come from sitting on a couch and doing nothing all the time.'

# 5

# STREAMLINE: MINIMISE THE FEARS

So far, the first two Ss have given you some practical suggestions of ways you can increase your resilience. But the third S is slightly different, because, as you'll have learnt by the end of this chapter, resilience is as much about what you *don't do* as it is about what you *do*.

I learnt this myself through my cancer. That experience definitely gave me tools and skills — things I could *do* — to make myself more resilient. But it also showed me what I needed to *not* do — behaviours that I had no idea were affecting me so negatively until I had stopped them, but which were actively harming my ability to be resilient.

.........

Looking back on my time at high school, there are a few key impressions or feelings which I think define that period of my life.

Firstly, there was the feeling of sheer joy of days when I didn't have to go to school on a usual school day: public holidays, teacher-only days, strikes, the occasional snow day.

The second feeling is a little harder to put into words, but it's about the excitement of that time of life. Lunchtimes laughing with mates. School dances. Walking to the shops and buying junk food after the bell rang. Bussing home with my headphones on, or later, once I had my restricted licence, driving myself home, typically via half of the city. Walking out of my final NCEA external for the year. Meeting mates at Macca's in the weekends, hanging around at the mall. Planning what we were doing for New Year's.

But my third memory from this time of life for me, the one which becomes particularly clear if I take an honest look back, is feeling worried about stuff. Seriously, I spent an alarming amount of time as a young person worrying about everything I could possibly worry about. Things like how swimming sports/cross country/athletics was coming up and I was going to have to fake being sick/bunk/come last in front of the whole school, or how a workbook for a subject was so thick I had no idea how we were going to get through it.

I laugh about these worries now, perhaps because they don't loom as large since facing cancer — or maybe I just grew out of them with time. But importantly, even though they seem trivial to me now, *they felt pretty bloody significant and real to me at the time*. I can honestly say I had more sleepless nights thanks to small worries like these than I ever had worrying about anything to do with cancer.

I spent much of my teenage years, to put it simply, worrying about dumb shit. And I realise now that not only did this make me miss out on some great times and prevent me from making the most of a really exciting time of life, but it also made me less resilient on a physiological (bodily) level.

.........

Research has shown that young people who worry a lot effectively *rewire their brains* to make themselves better at worrying and worse at problem-solving or solution-finding, setting themselves up to be less resilient for the rest of their lives. How is this possible? Well, I'm no neuroscience expert — but luckily I do know one.

Nathan Wallis is a neuroscience educator and an expert in how the brain works, develops and changes. His work focuses on how we can best prepare young people for the world by ensuring their brain develops in a way which sets them up to succeed. I find this idea pretty crazy, because it means there are things you can do as a teen (or younger) which develop your brain in ways which either benefit or harm you for the rest of your life.

One of those relates to anxiety and worry. We know from doing scans on the brains of teens that people who worry a lot can *change the way their brain grows*. There's a part of the brain called the amygdala which, for the sake of simplicity, we'll call the 'worry part' of the brain. There's another part called the prefrontal cortex, which is the solution-finding, problem-solving area — the part which, when something goes wrong, helps you find a way to deal with it.

Nathan explained that when it comes to young people who worry more, their brains basically say, 'Hey, since all this information which is coming in seems to end up in the worry part of the brain, why don't we build some new pathways or connections (called synapses) to allow the info to go straight there?' In doing so, they bypass the solution-finding part of the brain. You can actually see this on a scan: young people who worry a lot show physical changes in their brains that make them better at worrying and worse at problem-solving and solution finding. The worry part of their brain becomes dominant and controls their thought processes, which makes them more reactive and emotional and less resilient when confronted by adversity. Your body becomes really good at whatever you use it for; be that swimming, or singing, or netball — or worrying.

I find this terrifying — which ironically gives me another thing to worry about. There is some good news, though. Nathan explained that we also know that young people who can take their mind off their worries for at least part of the day don't suffer this same change. If you can tune out these worries for part of each day, your brain gets the rest it needs to prevent this change from happening.

Research has shown that as little as twenty minutes a day of consciously stopping turning your worries over in your head, taking some time out and practising deliberate, focused attention through an activity like meditation creates changes in the brain which make you more resilient. In fact, when I asked Nathan about his top advice for young people from the perspective of neuroscience, to help them become more resilient, his answer was clear:

> 'Young people today are living through a period of really rapid change, and their brains are trying to accommodate this by thinking really, really fast and taking on lots of information. Genetics normally take thousands of years to adapt to change, so you have to do something to counteract this fast-paced world we are in: stop thinking, focus on your breathing, and just slow down.
>
> 'If you think of yourself as having an internal motor, living in today's world is going to make that motor go fast, and that's going to be a recipe for anxiety and a low quality of life. You absolutely need to spend time each day slowing that motor down to be successful in this day and age.'

Hopefully, there are things you already do in your life which allow you to take your mind off the worry and stress for a while. I often ask students what allows them to mentally get away from life's worries, and their answers always surprise me. Whether it's playing sport, reading, writing, singing, spending time with family and friends, listening to music, walking the dog, or something else, chances are there are things you already do which allow you to decompress and not focus on your worries, or anything much at all, for a period of time. As a young person, it's incredibly important to try to build this time into every day — preferably an hour or two at least — to ensure your brain develops in a way which makes you as resilient as possible.

Of course, the other thing you can do is to try to overcome or eliminate as many of these worries as possible, because while it's great to be able to take your mind off them for a period of time each day, the best outcome would be having fewer things to worry *about*.

That brings us to the third S: Streamline. This is the idea of trying to minimise the fears, anxieties and worries which we all have on a daily basis *before* we encounter adversity, and then minimising your fears, anxieties and worries *during* adversity, to free up your brain to deal with the more pressing issues.

> **streamline (verb):** to design with a form that presents very little resistance to a flow of air or water, increasing speed and ease of movement; to alter in order to make more efficient or simple.

Either of these definitions creates a good mental image of why Streamlining is so important. In the simplest terms possible, as you face adversity throughout your life, you need to be mentally as light, agile, fast-moving and efficient — or Streamlined — as possible. All your extra fears and worries are baggage that simply slows you down and makes you less efficient. This is the first part of Streamlining — making sure that *before* adversity, you're as best prepared as you can be to get through it.

Offloading your fears *now* leaves you prepared for when the times do get tough, as they inevitably will. It's *preparation for resilience*, but it's just as important as all the other active steps of being resilient. If you can find ways to not worry so much about the smaller things, when bigger, less controllable things come along, you'll be in a better place to face them.

••••••••

Fun fact — out of all of the more than 100,000 young people I have worked with in the past nine years, across a handful or two of different countries, I have only ever come across three general fears or worries. Of course, I have talked with people about many hundreds of specific worries, but regardless of their background, country or culture, the worries over which we have any control can effectively be boiled down to three overarching fears:

1. Fear of the future
2. Fear of the small stuff
3. Fear of other people's opinions.

The fears over which I lost so much sleep when I was a teenager could be classified under those headings, too. But since having cancer, I don't really have any of those fears anymore — certainly not like I used to. Since those fears lost their hold on me, I've come to realise how much happier and more resilient I am in everyday life. That's why I want to talk about the three fears, and some of the lessons I've learnt which have helped me move past them, in the hope that they might apply to you as well.

## Fear 1: The Future

One of the defining elements of youth — at least according to the old people who drone on about it — is the seemingly limitless possibilities that lie ahead. I must've been told about fifty million times: 'The world is your oyster!' But as a teenager, my thoughts about the future were almost always saturated with a deep, stomach-churning sense of discomfort. Seriously, what the hell was I supposed to *do* with my life? The idea of having so many opportunities, so many possibilities lying ahead of me, felt far from exciting and empowering. Actually, it felt daunting and terrifying.

This is, in many ways, a completely new problem — and it's definitely a first-world one. It's worth remembering that, for many people your age around the world, leaving school (if you were lucky enough to have had a school to go to) and growing up doesn't mean having a whole bunch of opportunities; it means having to make pragmatic choices for you and your family to survive, or having no choices at all. But for most of you reading this, at the risk of sounding like one of those old people who proclaim just how much opportunity you have in front of you — they're completely right. In a very literal sense, our generation are the first people in history to have this much freedom at our fingertips.

For our parents, their parents, and certainly the generations before them, their futures were largely dictated to them by a range of factors out of their control: when and where they were born, what gender or race they were, what family they were born into. While some of these factors still have an effect today, through incredible shifts in access to knowledge, information, education and travel, leading to greater global connectedness, you genuinely have more options and opportunities than any one of your thousands of ancestors before you. So yeah, it's probably fair enough to feel a bit freaked out by it.

But the good news is, the reality of what's ahead is not as intimidating as it might feel when you're in the midst of it.

.........

Looking back at me and my mates in our final years of school, I'm shocked in equal measure by how adamant some of us were about what we wanted to do with our lives, and equally shocked by how little idea some of us had. Lots of friends were tossing up between vastly different fields, entirely unsure which one most appealed. It felt like some kind of life-threatening extreme sport: one incorrect move and things would be set in stone forever. It's also pretty alarming, looking back, that I was committed to spending five years and a small fortune studying law and commerce at university because I *sort of* thought it was *roughly* in an area which *kind of* interested me.

At the time, I felt like going to university was my only option, whereas I realise now that, for most young people, it's not. In my case, I would have actually been the first generation of my family to attend university straight after high school. My mum is a school principal and my father is a builder; they in turn came from families who worked extraordinarily hard to keep their heads above water and give their children the best opportunities they could. My dad was really keen that I go to university and not follow him into the building trade — perhaps because he could see what a hazard I was to myself and everyone in my vicinity on his building sites, standing on nails and falling off scaffolding.

I know lots of people who've been told by their parents that not only do they have to go to university but they must study to enter a profession such as medicine, law or engineering. Even though I did well at school, my parents didn't guide me into a professional career — I chose it for myself. My parents just wanted me to do what would make me feel happy and fulfilled, and although I am as reluctant as any young person to commend my parents, this was absolutely brilliant advice. I've seen the exact opposite play out for friends whose parents determined their path for them, and I'm thankful that wasn't what happened for me.

When I chatted with Chlöe Swarbrick for this book, this was something she echoed:

> 'Some of my friends went on to study accounting, and I said to them at the time, "But you hate accounting!", to which they replied, "Yeah, but my parents think it's a good job and it pays well." But if you hate accounting, and you're going to do that for forty hours plus of your week for the rest of your adult life, do you not think that angst will seep through into how you see the world and your life?'

Writer and mental-health advocate Jehan Casinader, who I also interviewed for this book, agrees:

> 'Lots of people go to university to "find themselves", and instead they just find themselves with a whole lot of debt and no real clue about what they want to do with the rest of their life. Meanwhile

> we're crying out for people in trades, and people who can innovate and take risks in many different industries. University can be a richly rewarding experience, and tertiary qualifications are very important in many sectors. But it isn't the only pathway to knowledge and success.'

You might want to go to university, polytech or another tertiary institution, and you might have an idea of what you want to study. Or, you might have lots of friends going to university and feel like you *should* go, too. Most schools have plenty of students who don't intend to go to university, or don't have it as an option. Only 40 per cent of Kiwi high-school students go straight from school to university, and universities around the country are seeing student numbers continuing to drop in recent years. In New Zealand, we also have one of the highest rates in the developed world of people dropping out of university once they've started studying — perhaps suggesting that too many people are starting down that path without considering if it's right for them.

There are many options open to you which do not involve tertiary study. Some of the most successful young people I've met are the people who didn't go to university straight away, or even at all. It's also okay to not know exactly what you want to do, and you can take your time to work it out. It's not a once-only opportunity to make the right choice.

As you get towards the conclusion of your high-school years, unless you're absolutely sure where your future lies, you need to keep your options open wide. Once you get into your final year, you need to actually engage some gears in your brain and decide what you want, and not just coast into a path without giving it much thought. This is the mistake I've seen a lot of people make — getting swept along by our conveyer-belt education system, which will often direct you into university unless you consciously and deliberately make a different decision.

You need to capitalise on what you have available to you, whether that's the opportunity to go to university, or get into a family business, or train for a trade. Maybe you have existing connections in a particular field, or just a knack for striking up conversation with people and finding out what's out there. Take the time to meet as many people as possible and be polite, humble and genuine with them, while also being upfront about what opportunities you are looking for, to see what connections you can make. For some careers, a tertiary qualification is essential — I wouldn't want a surgeon cutting me open without a qualification to prove he knows my knee from my kidney. But there are so many other opportunities to find a career that you both love and find satisfying.

Take me, for example: after my cancer, I've stumbled into being offered a few vastly different long-term career options, and I've been lucky that through my story and connections I've got that initial foot in the door. If you can find something or someone to help you get into that position — without taking the fairly drastic step of getting cancer — you'll be surprised by the possibilities and opportunities that turn up.

Since I left school, some of the greatest reassurance about the future and what it might hold has come from talking to adults, not just about their current career, but how they actually ended up doing it. I highly recommend you try it, because it's pretty entertaining and often not what you'd expect. Some of my recent conversations have included: 'Well, I was a professional lawn-turf layer for a few years [insert long and winding story here] . . . and so that's how I ended up becoming the winch operator on a rescue helicopter', and 'I started at uni studying veterinary medicine [insert long and winding story here] . . . and that's how I ended up organising concerts and festivals'.

Ask a few of the adults in your world how they ended up doing what they do. If they say they studied a subject at uni and went straight into that field (which seems to be more uncommon than not), ask how and why they ended up studying it. I've had people tell me they overheard a conversation in a café which piqued their interest, or found a book they started reading out of curiosity, or their school careers advisor just threw the suggestion out there and they went with it. People bump into someone who offers them a career change, they stumble into the wrong lecture hall, they do it for a bet — there are all sorts of great stories.

One which stuck out for me was when I chatted to All Black Will Jordan for this book. He told me, with a look of disbelief on his face, that he was actually planning to give up playing rugby when he was in year 12, 'but then the coach told me that I wouldn't be coming on the team trip to Japan if I did that, so I sort of decided to stick with it until after then.' One thing led to another, and he's now one of the best rugby players in the world.

•••••••••

The bottom line is that yes, these decisions, or moments, or coincidences, do have massive impacts on people's lives, as they will on yours. The realisation I had in my latter years of school that things were getting very real and very serious, very fast, was entirely correct. Yes, failing a subject can change where you work for the rest of your life. Yes, missing a careers appointment might alter your path as well.

But the reality, as evidenced by my own life, is that *none of these factors can really be controlled*. What happened to me was so out of left field that no one could have expected it. The things that will shape your path are entirely unpredictable. This is not something to be afraid of, however, because the story of every person I talk to about how their lives have turned out involves them standing in front of me chatting, happy and unwilling to have changed anything about that story, no matter how many twists and turns there had been along the way.

I can honestly say I've never met someone who told me they wished they hadn't taken an opportunity which had led them down their current path. Even in the interviews I have conducted for this book, one of the most crucial questions I've asked people is about what they would change, or what they regret, or what they would do differently about being a teenager if they had a second chance. Most people have told me some variation of 'there's nothing I would change, because if I changed something then I might not have ended up here, and I like it here'.

Since going into remission from my cancer, I've had the opportunity to build my own business, and to work with all sorts of groups — sports teams, businesses, governments, conferences and events, and schools. To write books, to travel to different places, and to present to audiences on my work.

I certainly haven't pursued a career in commerce and law, and, from what I've seen from my friends who did go down this track, I'm confident that I wouldn't have enjoyed it anywhere near as much as I enjoy what I've ended up doing. I probably would've been happy, and I guess I wouldn't have known any different, but I find it hard to picture life being any better than it is right now.

While in the past I battled feelings of self-doubt and helplessness, and tied myself in knots trying to come up with the 'right' path forward, the irony is that now I'm grateful to have fallen into this completely different path. If I could go back in time to high school, I would do everything I could to reassure myself that those feelings of worry weren't necessary.

There are a few reasons for this. Firstly, without being dramatic, I now realise that there I was in year 13, worrying about what I was going to do with my life, when all of a sudden I nearly died from cancer. I went from agonising about what majors to select at uni to lying around in hospital wondering if I'd even make it to university at all. Obviously, this is probably not going to happen to you, and I'm not just pulling the cancer card for effect. What I'm trying to say is that the best-laid plans can still go astray — and I actually find that reassuring. It means that in the grand scheme of things, 'major decisions' often turn out to be minor, and the things we can control are vastly outnumbered by the things we cannot.

I was so scared, so worried about how the future would turn out, kept awake at night worrying about how it could all go wrong — and all this anxiety was based on the possibility of choosing the wrong university courses. Then I was blindsided by possibly one of the worst things that could happen to me and nearly died . . . and the outcome was living a happier, more fulfilled life, in a career I could never have imagined but which I love. Things didn't just go wrong, they went far worse than anything I was worrying about — *and it all turned out brilliantly*.

This part of it is applicable to you, cancer or not:

> No matter what your fears of the future centre around, they are likely to be less important than many of the bad things which will happen to you in your life.

The odds are that when you look back, not only will you laugh at how minor the things you dreaded turned out to be, but you'll see that even when things went terribly wrong you still found the opportunity to smile, laugh and make the most of a bad situation (see chapter 4, Salvage, for more on this). The swirling motion of life which causes things to 'work themselves out' means you do not need to fear the future. Armed with the tools to be resilient and take on any adversity that comes your way, you will find your own path. Worrying about what that path might be isn't going to change it.

••••••••

We are all a product of all of the experiences we go through, both the good and bad. None of the people I've talked to about resilience have told me that their lives have been perfect, or that they haven't made massive mistakes along the way, or that they haven't been hurt — but none of them would change much, apart from *worrying less about how it would all turn out*.

This might seem unbelievable to you, but take it from the guy who wouldn't change the fact that he got cancer — it's true. Whether it's because things really do always work out for the best or, more likely, because humans possess a powerful drive to stop ourselves from feeling regret, we always seem to be happy with how things end up.

I see so clearly now, but I couldn't at the time.

That said, there are still a few things which strike me as really important *not to do*, because they will make it tougher to achieve an outcome you're happy with:

- Don't make the mistake of thinking, 'I don't need to give things my best crack because it'll probably work out fine anyway'. Sure, even if you bunk class, fail exams because you can't be bothered giving a shit, and laugh about doing so, life will probably still work out okay. But it's 100 per cent guaranteed to work out *better* if you give it 10 per cent extra effort.
- Don't decide to study something for money, prestige, because other people want you to, or because other people are doing it. I know that can be easier said than done, but ending up working towards a job you know you'll hate just because it's going to make you rich or make other people happy is one of the few surefire ways of buggering

everything up. Doing a job which pays well in a field you hate is a waste of your life.

- Even if you're lucky enough to have the opportunity, don't feel that you have to go university. Keep your options open and explore alternatives. Instead, capitalise on your contacts, connections and leaving good impressions on people you meet. Look around at opportunities you might not have considered. There's time to go to uni later if you want to — you don't need to just ride the conveyer belt straight through the front gates.
- Don't hold off on doing something because you're worried about rejection or because you don't think much of your chances of success. If in doubt, ask and you might receive. How do you think you ended up reading this book? I sent off the idea one day to a publisher and they said yes. Likewise, getting to interview the incredible people I've talked to for this book. Most good people want to help other good people, so use that to your advantage. Don't be afraid to make things happen for yourself.
- Don't worry about how everything will work out. As I've been saying, you can be completely set on going to uni and getting the best job in the world, then you might still get cancer out of the blue, like I did. Wait, that's making you worry more? Let me reword it: *there are many more things out of your control than in your control.* You're better off sailing with the tide instead of trying to fight against it. Relax and see where it takes you, while still using the rudder to have as much input as possible on your course.

> Just don't expect that you will necessarily end up where you thought you were going.

*Summarising Fear 1*

Sure, the future can feel big and scary. But seriously, so much of it is out of your control. Try not to drift along without thinking, do what you can to set yourself up for what you actually want to have happen, and then try to stop worrying. Easy, right?

## Fear 2: The Small Stuff

The second category of worry I find pops up when I'm talking to young people — and which dominated my own time at high school — is Small Stuff. By the way, when I talk about the small stuff, I'm not talking about earwigs crawling into your ears while you're asleep. I never thought I'd have to clear that up, until I gave a talk at a primary school on the West Coast, and at the end one boy put his hand up and asked me if that's what I meant by the 'small things'. It's not, although it's a new and exciting fear I might consider adopting.

So what *do* I mean by the 'small stuff'? Well, I can't actually think of specific examples of the little things I worried about when I was at high school — which is quite telling. I think I can't remember because, by definition, these things didn't really matter at the time, and they certainly don't now. I've long since forgotten them, because they turned out to have no importance or impact on my life today.

I remember big things like my nana getting cancer, or my parents splitting up, because it altered the course of my life (in both good and bad ways, as it turned out). But exams I flunked, assignments for which I got a grade lower than I'd hoped for, sports matches where I let the winning goal in or failed to deliver the winning kick, times I fell out with my mates or got left out . . . they're not taking up space in my memory anymore.

To be clear: when I talk about the small stuff, I know that it doesn't *feel* small at the time. The anxieties and fears which I often had growing up obviously all pale in comparison to the concerns I was suddenly facing when my cancer was diagnosed, but I can honestly say I lost more sleep worrying about swimming sports, how my skin had broken out, and upcoming exams than I ever lost to cancer or fearing death. I used to lie in bed at night ruminating — worrying about things, or going over and over mistakes I thought I'd made or ways in which I felt I had embarrassed myself. Some mornings I would wake up around 5 a.m. and not be able to go back to sleep — all because of these fears which, I realise now, *did not matter*. And regardless of whether they 'mattered' or not, worrying about them didn't do anything to fix, change or help them in any way — it was wasted time and energy.

I guess this is one of the biggest changes in me since my cancer. Put simply, since facing death, I generally find it much harder to get worked up about things which aren't on a life-and-death scale. I feel really fortunate that things which I think previously would have weighed me down now don't have that effect. As with all of these fears, this is me at my best, and not me always: I do still sometimes get worked up about minor or irrelevant things, fixate on small issues, complain and whinge about things which just don't matter in the grand scheme of things — but I do it far less than I did before cancer.

It's not that the cancer got rid of these worries, or even that it made me stop caring about them — it's just that it gave me a *point of reference* to compare them to, to consider just how much they really mattered. Because when you've checked out the alternatives first-hand (e.g. another day of chemo), everything looks pretty bloody good in comparison — even quite shitty things.

You know that feeling when you're getting over a cold or flu, and you wake up one morning feeling healthy and well again, absolutely fizzing because you're so happy to feel good again? Or when you nose finally unblocks and you've got the ability to breathe again and it's just mind-blowingly good because you're aware of it now? For me, coming through cancer was kind of like that, but on steroids. Particularly in the first little while after my treatment finished, every time I came up against something worrying or annoying, I'd compare it to cancer, and think, 'Phew, that's not so bad!'

Parking ticket? *Rather pay it than have to do another day of chemo.*

Missed a flight because I was stuck in traffic? *Better than missing it because I've had a relapse and am back in hospital.*

Had an argument with someone? *If I'm fighting with them, I'm still alive.*

I've gone through some tough times since the cancer, but nothing has passed the test of being worse than being back in hospital. This, for me, is what has enabled me to worry less about the things like parking tickets, missed flights and tiffs with people. I have this way to *put things into perspective* and work out how big or small they really are. My experience of cancer gave me a useful tool, a measuring stick to figure out whether or not things are worth worrying about:

> Is [insert shitty situation here] worse than being in hospital having chemo?

I haven't yet come up against anything which has made me say 'no'.

This is great for me — but how can *you* do this? With any luck, you can't ask yourself, 'Does this beat the time I had cancer?' Hopefully, you don't have any serious comparison point for when you are considering 'How bad is this really?' or 'How much does this actually matter?' So, what *can* you measure your worries against? How can you tell what matters, and what is just small stuff not worth wasting too much effort and energy on? It can be really difficult to gain some perspective on your worries and how significant they are while you're in the midst of them.

Good news: I think I've figured out a way.

.........

Back in late 2020, I was facing a pretty shitty time — as was pretty much everyone else around the world in the wake of the global pandemic. In my case, Covid and the subsequent border closures and travel restrictions had effectively shut down my business. I was stuck overseas, away from my family and with no certainty about when I would see them next. The life I had built for myself in the years prior to Covid seemed, without being dramatic, to be slipping away.

One afternoon, I was looking for something on my computer, when I came across an autobiography written by my partner Jem's grandfather, who had passed away in 2013. It had been forwarded to me about three years earlier and now, in my not-quite-unemployed but certainly under-employed state, I finally had the time to read it properly.

Jem's pop, John Morrissey, was an incredible man. Coming from humble beginnings, he attended the same high school as I had, alongside my grandfather and great-uncle. He excelled in sport and, after leaving school, climbed his way through the ranks to become an All Black, debuting in 1962. After that — not satisfied with reaching sporting heights to which most people can only ever aspire — he then started working his way up in the world of business. He became CEO of the Edmonds Group, then started his own business which employed hundreds of staff. Throughout this journey, he made a fortune, lost a fortune, and made an even bigger fortune. He went on to change people's lives via philanthropic pursuits such as funding the construction of Bev Morrissey House (named after his late wife and Jem's grandmother) for Hōhepa, a charity which provides support to intellectually disabled people, and building the First XV field grandstand at Christchurch Boys' High.

His life was truly an example of all-round success — sporting, business and entrepreneurial triumphs — topped off by using the wealth he had created to benefit others around him. More importantly, he was a good person and is remembered by others as such. It's no wonder he had called his autobiography *One Man's Dream Run*.

His life was, however, also touched by adversity, as all our lives inevitably are. As I read his life story, I could see that there had been as many downs as there were ups — sadness and heartbreak; challenges which must have seemed insurmountable at the time; massive levels of failure and loss.

But I began to notice that no matter how bad something was, it took up barely more than a page of his life story. The passing of a close friend would be summed up in a paragraph. Being unceremoniously dropped from the All Blacks covered a few lines. Catastrophic financial losses were captured in a sentence. But of all these life-altering, crushing, lie-awake-at-night-worrying problems, nothing took up more than a page or two. Never a whole chapter. When the scale of a whole life was considered, these issues were put into perspective — and they were a hell of a lot smaller than they must have felt at the time. I wondered if John realised this as he experienced them, or whether he only noticed as he wrote about them decades later. I wish I'd had the chance to ask him.

It got me thinking about my own problems at that time. I started to ask myself:

> In my life story, how much space will this problem take up?

Looking at the worries I was facing at the time — being indefinitely separated from my friends and family, and the loss, either temporary or permanent, of my business — I thought they would absolutely warrant a mention. But, on reflection, I didn't think they would get a page. I wasn't kidding myself: these things *were* important, but when I looked at them from this perspective, they weren't *that* important. In a life story covering eighty or more years of ups and downs, where would this time sit? At the lower end of the scale.

Then I started to wonder how far this rule could be applied. What would even make it into the book, and what wouldn't? That flat tyre the other day? Of course not. Broken phone screen? No. Getting cancer? Yes, that might actually get a chapter — not because of the adversity, but because of the positive impacts it had on my life.

Even looking back now and sketching the outline of what my life story might look like, of all the adversity I've been through, I know one thing for sure: I haven't yet experienced something so bad happening that it would take up more than a page or two in my story. Most of the things that come to mind might warrant a fleeting mention. But, and most crucially for this chapter, *all of the things I used to worry about on a daily basis during high school won't even get a single line in my life story.*

Now, this isn't about diminishing your worries. Like I said, I could recognise the fact that hey, the whole Covid thing was going to get a mention in the story of my life. I didn't try to write it off and tell myself to just get on with it. And the same goes for you: you may well face some challenges as a young adult which *will* make it into your life story when you write it one day. But you will face more and more challenges as time goes on, and you need to sort out which of them are worth worrying about and which ones aren't. The thing to continually ask yourself is:

> Will this warrant a mention in my life story?

If the answer is no, and it's not going to make the book, *you'd be better off not dedicating so much of your time and effort to worrying about it.* It's bad for you emotionally, it's bad for your brain development, it's just a bad way to spend your time. Worrying about small things is just a waste of time and energy.

.........

Even though I feel I've got a pretty good perspective on my worries from going through the cancer, something about John's story left me with a whole new level of calm and optimism. I could see the ups and downs in his life, and how the downs didn't prevent the ups, and how even the biggest downs ended up being just small passages of text as he looked back over his life story. The same applies to the life story of anyone you admire or look up to. In their 'books' — and, for many successful people, the literal books about their lives — so many of the failures and worries they encounter along the way turn out to be inconsequential and hardly worthy of mention.

Looking back to when I was a teenager, I think that if I had measured my worries against this 'life story' test, I would've worked out a lot more quickly what was worth worrying about — and what wasn't. If I had been able to do that, I think I would've enjoyed that time of life far more, and been far better prepared to face the real challenges which came my way.

At the very least, if I wasn't able to completely disregard these worries, I wish I had learnt from them. After all, day-to-day adversities are absolutely critical to us learning and growing as human beings, because they act as a training ground to practise resilience and develop all of the skills and tools in this book. In that sense, small challenges are an opportunity.

Jehan Casinader remembers how enormous the small stuff seemed when he was a teenager, and how he's had to learn to keep things in perspective:

> 'As you get older, you realise how insignificant many of your problems are. I'm in my thirties now, and when I look back at the things I was losing sleep over in my teens — or even last month — I can see that most of them just don't matter.'

It's important to note that when the small stuff begins to feel bigger and bigger — bigger than it ought to or bigger than it used to — that can be a warning sign for your mental health. Feeling overwhelmed by the small stuff — when minor issues, things which you recognise don't really matter that much, begin to feel impossible to overcome, or you feel as though you can't see a way through them — can be an early warning sign that it might be worth talking to someone about what's on your mind.

This tendency to notice small worries isn't just something which happens in our teenage years, nor is it a fault or failing in some way. Rather, it is just how we are geared as humans: we have developed a natural ability to recognise and remember the bad things which happen to us far more easily than the good things, because throughout our evolution, we've needed to recognise and remember the things which are bad to keep ourselves safe. If, back in the Stone Age, you didn't remember dangerous things — what plant was poisonous, or where the dangerous animals liked to hang out — then you didn't survive to have children, and your genes didn't get passed down. The people who could recognise and remember bad things were the ones who survived. So fixating on small problems doesn't make us negative people; it just makes us human.

The truth is, though, that for all the bad things which happen to us in any given day — and I'm not talking about *really* bad things, I'm talking day-to-day problems here — there are *many, many times more good things*. This isn't philosophical nonsense, either — this is pure mathematical fact. Let me tell you how I figured it out. Let me tell you about Kane.

.........

I don't have a lot of really special possessions. If someone asked me, 'What would you grab if your house was burning down?', I'd say something as boring as 'my passport', and maybe my laptop. If it was a slower-moving fire, I might start scooping up things like my carbon-fibre road bike (it wasn't cheap, and it might aid in my escape from the fire anyway). And then I would grab my mug.

Everyone has a favourite mug, and if they don't, then they should. Mine is a little battered, having been used every day for the best part of the last five years. On the front it has the words 'Heart of Gold', and a picture of a teddy bear holding up a heart which used to be gold but has long since faded after many cycles through the dishwasher. It has little hearts scattered around the outside, and a neat row of multicoloured ones on the inside of the lip, which I use to gauge how much milk I put in my tea. This is my mug from Kane.

In the years since I went into remission, I've connected with a number of people who have either been diagnosed, or their child has been diagnosed, with the same cancer I had. Burkitt lymphoma is so rare that I'm often the only person they have ever heard of to have had it. Through this, I've had the chance to meet maybe a dozen other patients and their families. One of those was Kane.

When I first met Kane, he was only eleven years old and had been diagnosed with Burkitt's about two weeks earlier. I showed up to CHOC, the Children's Haematology and Oncology Centre (effectively the under-eighteen version of the BMTU), to meet him and his family one cold winter's afternoon. Kane had only just started his treatment, still had a full head of hair, and was responding well. He was mostly concerned about his chances of being able to play football again and missing his friends from school. As we talked, I was blown away by this young guy's maturity, facing a battle greater than most people will ever face with a cool and calm resolve. His little sister, Aliya, climbed over him and pleaded for his attention with the adoration a much younger sister has for her older brother.

We talked about football, and treatment, and what to expect; that things would be tough and that despite it, he would get through. I answered some of his questions about what the treatment and some procedures were like. I also spoke privately with his mum, and assured her that although it was going to present an enormous challenge to both Kane and his family, they would get through it, and Kane would be just fine.

Kane's treatment progressed well, and I visited him whenever I was back in Christchurch, watching as the cancer and chemotherapy shrunk his body into the shape of a very sick kid, stealing his hair and spare fat and muscle but never his steely resolve and bravery. And a few months later, he had done it: he had beaten his cancer, been told he was in remission, cleared to go out and begin moving on in his life. He would be home with his family in time for Christmas — which would have to be the best Christmas ever, right? He had a hell of a lot ahead of him, especially relative to the comparatively small amount of years he had behind him.

There are a couple of traditions in CHOC when you're told you are in remission. Firstly, you get to ring a large silver bell — the remission bell. Its clangs echo around the corridors of the ward and spread joy, celebration and, most importantly, hope, to other patients, families and staff. It's a hell of an honour to get to ring the bell, because it's no small achievement to earn the right to do it. Kane rang the bell.

The second tradition is writing your name on the giraffe which stands by the door to CHOC, like some kind of bouncer or long-necked guard dog. Kane wrote his name right on the tip of the giraffe's nose — exactly where I would've, too. Then he left CHOC and headed home with his family.

But just over a month later, on 20 December, Kane was brave enough to tell his mum that he had pain in his stomach again, where the cancer had first been found. It was straight back into hospital for CT scans and an urgent biopsy. Two days later, the oncologist confirmed the cancer had recurred. Chemo resumed immediately. Kane's response? 'Don't worry, Mum — it means I'll get to ring the bell twice.'

The second round of chemo was initially effective, but not fully. Kane then had major surgery to remove a tumour mass. He was a good candidate for a bone-marrow transplant — a treatment which can often save a life. Fortunately, his sister Aliya was considered a close-enough match to donate her stem cells, in a lifesaving manifestation of her love for Kane. However, as the transplant date approached, Kane's health deteriorated. His right kidney became blocked, and the doctors found the blockage was cancerous, too.

In the days after this blockage was found, I caught up with Kane and his mum for coffee, which then became a trip to Timezone. It was brilliant — not only am I still at a level of maturity where Timezone can be the highlight of my day, but it meant that Kane was out of hospital and back in the real world, doing normal stuff for a kid of his age.

At one point over our coffee, his mum talked to me about what the blockage meant for Kane's prognosis. I don't recall how it happened, but through a combination of deliberately chosen words and intense eye contact, on perhaps the third or fourth time it was sent across the table, I finally received the message: Kane had reached the end of the road in his treatment. This time, he would not be ringing the bell.

In that moment I felt the same way I'd felt when I was told of my own cancer: completely numb. I stammered and stumbled, trying to think of what to say. I often wonder if people expect me to know what to say when it comes to things to do with cancer, given my own experience. I don't. I still find myself scrambling for words that I don't have, just as much as I used to before cancer was a huge part of my world. Is there even anything to say?

After this conversation, we spent another hour or so at Timezone, where I took Kane on in bowling, Mario Kart, anything we felt like. Maybe you picture this being a tragic scene, but it truly wasn't. I've certainly never had a more meaningful experience at Timezone. I savoured that hour with gratitude that can't be put into words. Then I left, and walked around Hagley Park for an hour trying to understand if it was really possible, and if so, *how* it could be possible that a child could die from cancer before even having a chance to leave school.

It seemed an abomination of nature, an impossibility, so wrong that it should theoretically not be able to happen. Someone would prevent it, make it stop, because that was the only reasonable action to take. I knew that I was never going to die from my cancer; I truly didn't think Kane could either.

But Kane did die. He died on 24 May 2019. He died a young man, robbed of the chance to progress any further.

••••••••

Two weeks later, I caught up with Kane's mum again. She was the embodiment of strength and resilience, profound and wise and wholly selfless in the loss of her son. I came away inspired that someone could display such powerful inner strength.

Over coffee, she gave me a gift: a mug with the words 'Heart of Gold' on the front, and a card signed by the whole family, including Kane in his absence. That mug instantly became one of my most treasured possessions.

For me, that mug has been a powerful tool ever since — not only for drinking tea, but to help me enjoy my life a whole lot more. It puts me in the mindset to not only disregard the small issues I'm facing, or the ways people have annoyed me, or the stresses which are weighing on my mind, but it also reminds me to *watch for the good things* in that day, no matter how small they are.

Some mornings, I boil the jug and fill the mug, step outside onto my balcony and look around. I think about how grateful I am to be alive. I feel the sunshine coming down on my skin and think about the people who are still stuck in the BMTU, or CHOC, unable to step outside their door and suck in some fresh air and feel sunlight on their skin. I think about all the endless possibilities which lie ahead for me — all the opportunities, all the goodness which is available to me. I think of Kane.

For me, the mug is about *gratitude*. It's about capturing the small wins, about optimism. Even on the shitty days, it's a reminder *just how much better this is than the alternative*. Thank you for that reminder, Kane.

*Summarising Fear 2*

I believe that every one of us has a 'small things' switch. The switch is either set to 'capture small wins' or 'capture small losses'. You can't do both — you can't be looking around at all the things you appreciate and still feel slighted by all of life's small troubles, which weigh on us all. Likewise, if you're fixated on all of the things that are (or could go) wrong, you're going to miss a lot of what's going right in your day.

You have to choose one or the other. Choose to capture the small wins and you'll let go of the small losses. Or even just choose to use the 'life story' measure to help you to let go of the small losses, and I promise you'll start to notice the small wins you get every day as well.

## Fear 3: Other People's Opinions

The third category of fear is the fear of other people's opinions — yet another thing I also suffered from throughout my time at school. My teenage years were a prolonged period of self-doubt and generally feeling uncomfortable about everything I said, what I did, what I wore, who I was.

Call it whatever you want: insecurity, self-doubt, self-consciousness, lack of confidence. When I look back on that time of my life, I just remember feeling uncomfortable most of the time, worried about what other people thought of me, whether they liked me, things they had said to me. I felt like I was walking on eggshells when I chose my actions, words, activities, all driven by a fear of being 'uncool'. At the time, I think I felt like a relatively free person, able to make choices based on what I wanted to do, but in reality I was actually becoming a person based on the opinions of my peers, what social media said was cool, and basically whatever I didn't get shit for from other people.

This pattern of altering your behaviour to appease the opinions of other people is incredibly common among young people. But it's also incredibly unhelpful, and can have a really big impact on your overall wellbeing and resilience.

It's important to explain early on that when I talk about other people's opinions, there's a very specific type of opinion I'm talking about. Opinions can either be made up of advice (as in a 'professional opinion' — someone's meaningful and informed input or contribution), or judgement (which is just someone's personal feeling or thoughts about a topic or an action, which are typically not helpful). An opinion which is advice might be your careers advisor telling you that you're great at maths, physics and graphics, so perhaps architecture might be something which would interest you. An opinion which is judgement would be your careers advisor telling you that your shoes were ugly — 'What the hell were you thinking? Did you get dressed in the dark this morning?' They are two very separate things, and it's worth noting that when I talk here about other people's opinions, I'm talking about the *judgement* of other people and not their advice (especially in areas where they have relevant expertise).

This idea of moulding yourself to suit the opinions of the people around you, rather than who you want to be, is the kind of thing your parents and teachers tell you not to do — giving in to 'peer pressure'. They are worried that you will 'fall in with the wrong crowd' if you are unable to stand on your own two feet and make your own calls, instead being led by the people around you. But having been a teenager who constantly worried about other people's opinions, I know that making your own decisions is much easier said than done.

There is some good news, however. Things change — and hopefully get better — as you get older. As a young person, following the crowd is largely just a method of survival. I'm not suggesting that as a fourteen-year-old I ever wanted to or should have rebelled against all that was considered 'cool', and instead forged my own path, whatever that might have been. But forging your own path becomes easier and easier to do, and for you to be whatever you want, the further through life you get: the difference between the freedom you have to be yourself in high school and after it, at university or in the workforce, is worlds apart. Today, as an adult, I could show up anywhere, wearing whatever I wanted, and get through most days without much more than a raised eyebrow (and certainly not cop the judgemental comments I would have at school). That is the beauty of growing up and moving into the 'real world', where people have learnt to just get along and tolerate each other regardless of their differences (sort of, for most people, most of the time).

The way you may feel isolated or marginalised at school has a solution or at least an improvement on the horizon, however hard it might be to see at the time. At the very least, the judgement you face from your peers and society at large will reduce the further through life you get and the more people you interact with. While you might feel there are very few people like you at school, outside those gates and in your adult life you can choose to surround yourself with people who you have lots in common with and who make you feel as though you fit in.

I definitely wouldn't have had the guts to do what I do now back when I was at high school. I found receiving any attention at school really tough, so it would've been a real stretch to get up on a stage in front of strangers for a job, or put myself out there through the book you're reading right now. I had to have overcome my fear of other people's opinions first, and it's just as well I did, because public speaking, I can assure you, doesn't always go to plan.

As an example, I once thanked my hosts for inviting me to be part of their 'ostentatious occasion', without having a particularly firm grasp on what ostentatious meant. (No, I'm not sure why I did that either.) After a few audience members made interesting faces, a quick google informed me I'd basically said, 'Thanks, you snobby pricks, for the invitation to attend today and listen to you all give yourselves a big pat on the back, since you reckon you're so bloody cool.' Brilliant. Anyway . . .

In spite of occasions when things like this have gone wrong, I don't suffer from nerves before I get up to present at schools or conferences or workplaces (although I wonder if instead, audience members now suffer from nerves that their guest speaker is going to insult them). The whole 'do you get nervous?' thing is a question I get asked often, and when I explain that I don't, the other person usually asks if I calm my nerves by using the clichéd trick of imagining the audience naked — and I tell them that, given I speak mostly at schools, no, I actually don't do that.

The real reason that I don't get nervous when I speak in public is a little more complex, but it certainly deserves an explanation, because it has been one of the most significant forces shaping my life and one of the greatest benefits of having gone through cancer.

When I was going through my treatment for cancer, my body changed a lot. I lost a lot of weight, which left me looking emaciated, hollowed out, like a skeleton with skin stretched over it. I just looked sick — so sick it was uncomfortable to look at me. I also had a distinct lack of hair, ranging from the stuff on the top of my head, to my eyebrows, to my leg hair, to everything else. Losing my eyebrows was the worst — you can put a beanie on top of your bald dome, but covering your eyebrows requires a balaclava, which makes shopping difficult and visits to banks downright risky. I looked very strange, both to other people and in my own eyes. I looked into the mirror and saw an entirely unfamiliar, clearly very ill face looking back at me. It made me feel, initially, very self-conscious.

When you're that sick and you go out in public, people do stare. Wearing a beanie in summer, combined with looking that unwell, means you naturally attract attention. Not in a malicious way — people looked at me with sympathetic eyes, and they would often smile — but, as insecure as I was in that state, attracting any form of attention was the last thing I wanted.

Being newly bald was far from the only awkward, embarrassing situation cancer put me in. There was the time I was boarding a flight using crutches because of nerve damage in my legs, when the flight attendant playfully asked, 'Oh no, what have you done to yourself?' My mum snapped back, 'He got cancer!' Cue awkward silence. There were plenty more moments throughout cancer where I just wanted the ground to swallow me up. At least, there were at first, until one moment in particular changed all that, and the rest of my life.

........

One afternoon I was lying in my hospital bed after a particularly tough morning of treatment: a few bags of chemo, perhaps a spinal injection as well, and I was feeling pretty rough. Imagine the worst bug you've ever had, then making it much worse, and then tripling it. I had so little energy, even rolling over in bed felt impossible. Too hot and yet too cold all at once, sweating and shivering simultaneously. The world felt like one of those dreams which doesn't quite make sense, leaving me with a sense of unease that something was going horribly wrong.

There I was, staring at the ceiling, sweating and shivering and feeling like I couldn't imagine being more uncomfortable. I was mentally grappling with nausea — the nurses had a wide variety of pills which would help, and all I had to do was ask — but some days I felt more sick of being reliant on other people than I felt sick of feeling sick, so instead I lay there and used my mind to fight my stomach.

As I lay there trying to outthink the nausea, the nausea

outthought me, and I rather unexpectedly cascaded vomit down my front, all over my clothes and all through the bedding. I distinctly remember thinking, 'Yep, I really am laying here right now in a pool of my own vomit', which felt bemusing at first and then, straight after, I felt a real sense of sadness.

I was physically too weak to move. I was literally unable to get up — and even if I could, what was I going to do? Strip the bed and run to the local laundromat? Take off my blue and white (and now orange and yellow) hospital gown and run naked out of the hospital to the nearest Hallensteins to pick up some new basics? There was nothing to do except lay around in my vomit, or buzz the nurses for help. So I grabbed my buzzer and rolled my thumb around the edge of the nurse-call button until I felt bold enough to press it.

After a while, a nurse came. She was entirely unsurprised, or kind enough to act as though she was. I was in a chemo ward after all, so this must happen occasionally, right? Right? In that moment, however, that wasn't my reasoning.

Believe it or not, I couldn't think of the right way to say, 'Look, I've thrown up in the bed, and I'm going to need you to clean it up and then clean me up and help me get changed because I can't do that for myself', so when she opened the door I just sat there in miserable silence. She, on the other hand, was kind and cheery — which, as everyone who has had someone be extremely kind to them when they were feeling sad knows, just makes you feel even more sad.

As well as being extraordinarily kind and caring, this nurse was young — only a few years older than me at the time. And, well, she was really quite pretty. While I had no romantic interest in her, having a cute member of the opposite sex, around the same age as me, who was a complete stranger, cleaning up my vomity bed sheets and hospital gown, all while treating me with nothing but kindness, was pure, unadulterated hell.

As I lay there, the sense of disaster continued to rise. I could feel my face getting hot and tears starting to well up as I clenched my jaw. Inside, I was stretching like a balloon. What the hell? How did I end up in this situation? What would my friends think if they saw me now? What the hell must this poor nurse think? I'm like a child, incapable of even caring for myself.

Suddenly, inside me something snapped. The balloon popped, and this thought sprang into my mind, with anger and resignation:

> Well then, it's lucky I don't care what anyone thinks about me, because if I did, this would be a really shitty situation.

A switch clicked in my head.

I started to process the thought that my brain had just spat out, like in the movies when the head of the crisis team snatches the piece of paper out of the printer and begins to frantically read it.

> If I don't care what other people think about me, then this doesn't matter.
>
> Nor does my bald head, or my beanie in summer, or my lack of eyebrows, or my sickly-looking face and body. Nothing about this would be a problem anymore.

> All I have to do is not care what other people think, and move past it.

Straight away, my mind fired back another thought:

> But you have to care about what other people think, because otherwise you might do the wrong thing! Your concern about other people's opinions makes you do the right thing — otherwise everyone would just do whatever they wanted!

I mulled this over. Well, that was the answer then. I couldn't take the easy solution and just give up on what other people thought of me. That would be wrong, reckless, dangerous.

But the more I thought about it, I realised that wasn't really how I felt at all. Wearing a beanie, or not. Being bald, or not. Being ashamed of how I looked, or not. None of these scenarios involved *doing the wrong thing*. None of them was me *doing a bad thing*.

> None of this pressure, or fear of other people's opinions, was keeping me from doing something I shouldn't do — it was just making me feel like shit inside.

So, if there were no scenarios relating to my cancer where fearing other people's opinions was keeping me on the 'straight and narrow', were there any other scenarios where that might apply? Maybe playing up, being irresponsible or taking unnecessary risks, or being reckless with alcohol or drugs.

It was then I had my biggest epiphany yet:

> These weren't scenarios in which other people's opinions kept most people from doing the wrong thing. Rather, it was the complete opposite!

As a young person, I had seen my friends and peers do all sorts of stuff because other people had egged them on and they were too scared *not* to: stealing things, bullying people as part of a group, giving in to peer pressure. Rather than creating better people, bound by some kind of societal expectations or pressure to be a good person, a fear of other people's opinions was actually pushing me and my peers *away* from the right choices, and into doing things with negative consequences.

The more I thought about it, the less it made sense. Was fear of what other people thought really what kept me and my mates from robbing an old lady, for example? If the idea came to mind — which it hadn't — would the sole thought which stopped us be, 'Oh no, I can't do that, what will people say about me? They might call me the granny-robber! How embarrassing!' I think not. Likewise for parking in a disabled space, or pushing in front of someone in a queue — it wasn't other people's opinions which would stop me.

> It is our inner voice — our own values and morals — which guides those decisions.
>
> It is values and morals which steer people away from the wrong choices in tough situations — rather than the social

> pressure of fear of other people's opinions, opinions which instead often push them into wrong choices.

So then, what was the harm in opting out of this whole 'opinion-worry, self-conscious, choose-my-actions-based-on-other-people' thinking? What was the harm in saying loudly and proudly, 'I do not care what other people think about me'? Who would be hurt by it?

No one, as it turned out. In that moment I decided to try to stop worrying about other people's opinions as much as possible.

This, then, is the answer to the question 'Why don't you get nervous when public speaking?' The short answer is because I try not to care what other people think about me. Their opinions don't worry me, and because of that, I have nothing to fear from public speaking: I could get up on stage and completely butcher my speech — or, worse yet, call everyone in the room 'ostentatious' without knowing what it meant — and I can still walk out of the room with my head high, because I don't fear their opinions. Of course, I would never intentionally offend anyone, or hurt them, or let them down. But if they don't like me? That's okay, I don't mind.

I get that people might think this sounds arrogant. This comes back to the social contract we seem to believe in — that it is the fear of other people's opinions which keeps everyone from doing terrible things, and that to opt out of being concerned about them is to become a reckless, dangerous, unstoppable force of potential evil. But as I've said above, this is not how things work at all.

••••••••

As time has gone on, I've developed more nuanced checks and balances to guide my decision-making than just not caring what other people think of me, and I'll discuss those soon. But in that moment, laying in a sad puddle of vomit while waiting for a pretty nurse to come and save me, I had stumbled onto a strategy which has gone on to change my life for the better. It's just not caring *so much*.

This is not to be confused with complete disregard or deliberate shunning of social constructs like the need to wear clothes at the shops or shower occasionally. Nor does it mean expecting that other people will treat you any differently: you are simply disregarding their judgement, not making it go away. People will still judge you, still make snide remarks, laugh at you, treat you poorly. The difference is that whatever they do is entirely irrelevant, *because it doesn't affect you.*

Critically, this still leaves you with control over what you choose to do — and that doesn't mean you have to take the choice which most greatly disregards the opinions of others. For instance, even after my vomit-soaked revelation, I still chose to wear a beanie in public: it made *me* feel more comfortable, which was now a choice which I had made for *me*, as opposed to in the past when I felt like it was my only option to hopefully minimise unwanted attention. Easy.

This strategy came in quite handy over the following months of treatment. One night, when the nerve damage in my legs was at a bad stage, Jem and I went for dinner at an Italian restaurant in town. After our meal, Jem went to pay and left me at the table, so I didn't have to struggle my way over to the till. To get ready for our departure, I tried to get up. I took one step, then fell flat onto the wooden floor, incredibly effectively converting my gravitational potential energy into an extraordinarily loud bang. Every person, at every table, looked up from their pasta and pizza to observe the person they'd probably assumed had just dropped dead. ('Waiter, I'll have whatever he didn't have.') There were vague noises of embarrassment and even some tsking from the crowd as I wobbled around trying to get my feet under me for what felt like a lifetime, but was actually more like ten seconds — particularly since I suspect that quite a few of the other diners assumed I had overindulged in a few limoncellos. Once again, my new-found skill of caring less about what other people thought of me saved me from crippling shame.

Beyond these stories, and the many more cringeworthy situations I have been in since then, the greatest benefit to have come from this has not been the embarrassment I've been spared, *but the freedom I've had to be my own person and not have my choices shaped by others*. I look back on the years (and even months) prior to my diagnosis and subsequent vomit-puddle epiphany, and clearly see where my choices, actions and behaviours were shaped by other people's opinions.

I don't hold this against myself — I can't, because at the time, I didn't know any better — but I realise now I could have been a better person, and made a better go of that time of my life, if I could have let go of that fear. I can also see how I fell into the trap of being pushed or pressured into doing some things which could have got me into more serious strife — something I've seen happen first-hand plenty of times.

In case you think it's just you and me, even top sportspeople like Paralympian Liam Malone suffer from these same feelings and thoughts growing up. Liam reflects:

> 'The issue wasn't with other people judging me or giving me a hard time — the issue was that I wasn't confident and comfortable enough inside to be myself and move past their judgement.'

So, what exactly is this process that I use to guide my decision-making, now that I don't base it on the opinions of other people? What system of checks and balances do I have in place to ensure that I make the right calls?

As you might have picked up on, my decisions are largely guided by my *values and morals* — the things which I feel are important to me to model and display as a person. I'll go into this in much more detail in chapter 7, but some of my personal values are *optimism*, *loyalty*, *gratitude*, *growth*, *happiness* and *resilience*. These aren't even things I'm necessarily particularly good at — it's more a list of things I *want* to be good at. Everyone's list will be different, but there will be certain key values that stand out for each person.

Based on my own list of values, I use one key question to guide myself in the choices and decisions I have to make: will this further my pursuit of these values? If the answer is yes, then I do it.

> By measuring my decisions based on my own values and morals, I consistently make choices which align with not only who I am now, but who I want to become. Each

> choice I make brings me closer to being the version of myself I want to be.

There's something really reassuring about that — it's hard to second-guess your decisions when you know that you're truly just doing your best to be a good person. There's also the added benefit that the negative opinions of others seem to slide off your back even more easily when you remind yourself that you did what you truly felt was right. No one else can bugger up your choices for you, and you certainly don't have anyone else to blame for anything you get wrong.

At the end of the day, the bottom line for me is *if you do what you believe to be right, and what aligns with your values and morals, you have nothing to fear*, because you know you did the right thing in the moment, regardless of how things turn out. You can only make the best decision you can at the time. I guarantee that you'll never regret a decision that you made based on what you thought was right, and which aligned with your values.

........

So, that's the first part of the answer to the question 'What should my decisions and actions be guided by?' Your values and morals, which you might already know, or which you can learn more about in chapter 7.

The second part of the answer might seem a little bit contradictory: listening to the opinions of other people — but only a *very* select group of people.

To say I don't care about anyone's opinion of me isn't 100 per cent true — the people who are closest to me matter so much that to not care what they think about me is impossible. We instinctively care about the opinions of those closest to us, because we care about them.

For me, I care about the opinions of my family and some of my closest friends — and that's about it. I'm happy for them to have this role, because I trust them, and because they serve as my safety net. Even within that select group, there are people or groups whose opinions I give differing amounts of attention to, especially on different topics.

Your values can act as a compass to direct you in your decision-making: a constant and reliable force which, regardless of external pressures and forces, will allow you to clearly chart your pathway into the future. They can be an internal tool to help you measure your direction.

However, there is also a scientific phenomenon known as *magnetic deviance*, in which compasses are misdirected or their readings artificially altered by the ship's own magnetic field, and as a result they can give an incorrect reading. Ships, which in the pre-GPS era relied greatly on compasses for navigation, developed complex systems of counter-magnets to account for these changes — which is unsurprising when you consider that if you set off from Wellington headed for a beach party in Chile, and bugger it up by just one single degree, you'll end up in Antarctica instead. What I'm saying is, even compasses can be misguided and affected by external forces — and so can your moral compass.

Some of these external forces which are powerful enough to affect your moral compass are big things like love, wealth, power or fame. For example, maybe you have the chance to do something which you usually wouldn't because it doesn't align with your values, but you find yourself considering it because you could make a lot of money by doing it. Or you're asked by someone you love to do something you usually wouldn't because it doesn't align with your morals, but because you care so much about that person, you're prepared to do it.

> Just because money or love or power is a factor, it does not mean that your morals or values should bend to accommodate choices or decisions you would not make if they were not factors.

Your morals are one of the few things in your life that you ought to be inflexible on at all times, regardless of whether that appears to be to your success or detriment in the moment. Otherwise, this whole strategy falls apart — if your moral compass is willing to spin in any direction at any moment, based upon what appears to be in your favour at the time, it's entirely useless as a navigation tool for life.

Much like ships used to use this complex system of counter-magnets to account for magnetic deviance, you may need to apply some critical thinking in situations where your choices relate to love, money, power, fame or success. Sailors had to remain on the lookout for the deceptive forces that could alter their direction of travel, and likewise, the risk of moral magnetic deviance is that you will *be unaware of it unless you deliberately search for it.*

When these situations arise, ask yourself some searching questions, and answer them honestly. Would my choice be the same if money was not a factor? Is this a decision I can be comfortable with even if it goes wrong or things don't pan out as I expect? Through asking these questions, you can use your own counter-magnet system to balance out and account for possible influence of external factors on your morals, and subsequently on your decisions.

This is also where the opinions of those key people closest to you come into play, acting as a safety net. Those who know you best are best positioned to give you feedback on whether or not your decisions are truly aligned with you as a person and your values, and consequently they are a crucial resource to lean on during times of complex decision-making. They are the people best placed to keep you aligned on your true course, and to be able to give you a gentle nudge if you begin to drift off your desired path. The people who are closest to you will be able to keep you humble, grounded and doing the right thing and, for that reason, it's important to take their opinions into account — but only theirs.

Sometimes, it can be really tricky to find people trustworthy enough to fulfil that role for you — your friends or people you're close to mightn't actually be the best people for you to take advice from, even if you love them. Sometimes, your family and especially your parents might have their own biases or beliefs which they can project onto you, intentionally or unintentionally.

Also, we all grow and change, and sometimes we outgrow the people around us on our road to becoming a better person. For that reason, it's important to try to surround yourself with people who are better than you, people you aspire to be like (I'll discuss that more in chapter 6).

The reality is, however, that you will always care about the opinions of those closest to you — it's very difficult not to. For that reason, it's important to be conscious and aware of that, and to try to use it to your advantage, to remain true to yourself and who you want to be.

### *Summarising Fear 3*

- Don't allow your actions to be changed or decided by the opinions of other people. Instead, choose a selection of morals and values which you aspire to live by, and base your decisions on what best aligns with those values.
- As well as being guided by those values, find a core group of people around you to keep you grounded and true to yourself.
- If you do those two things, you'll be hard pressed to ever regret a decision, because you'll always know you did the right thing in the moment.
- Instead of worrying about other people's opinions and how to influence that perception, spend that time and energy on enjoying what is an amazing time of life.
  I know you're sick of being told, but being young means having the most opportunities at your fingertips that you

will ever have. To spend that time distracted by other people's opinions is to risk wasting it. I can confirm from experience that life is a whole lot better without being weighed down by other people's opinions.

- To allow yourself to change who you are to please other people, and to do things which don't feel right to you, is setting yourself up for regret down the line — and there will be no one to blame but yourself.

## Abbas Nazari — Making the Most of Opportunities

Abbas Nazari is a refugee, a bestselling author, a keynote speaker, a Fulbright Scholar, the owner of two successful gyms, and a father — all before the age of thirty. What is even more remarkable is the journey he took to get to this point.

I'm mindful of boxing Abbas in with how I define him, which is why I asked how he defines himself. 'I describe myself as a pretty determined individual. I'm focused clearly on my goals. I wear a number of different hats, be it in my personal or professional life. But most importantly, I don't let any of these things become my defining feature — each of these pieces form a whole.'

Abbas was born in Afghanistan, in an isolated village called Sungjoy, in the central highlands of the country. The first years of his childhood were peaceful — Afghanistan, at this time, did not carry the burden of war and destruction. His family lived in a mudbrick house in a truly idyllic setting, which he compares to the geography and landscapes of Central Otago, and he and his siblings attended school and played in the same carefree way we all do at that age. Life wasn't cushy, Abbas is at pains to stress — 'there was no running water, no power' — but his family lived a life of subsistence and simplicity that they enjoyed.

Their relaxed way of life was helped, to some degree, by the geographic isolation of their home. When Taliban radicals took over the capital, Kabul, and continued to spread their extremist ideology across the country, Sungjoy was only minimally impacted at first. It was only as time went on that word of the repression and intolerance began to reach Abbas's village.

Afghanistan is a patchwork quilt of different tribes and ethnic groups, all with different languages and beliefs. Abbas and his family belong to a group known as the Hazara people, a minority ethnic group which have been persecuted for centuries. As Abbas describes it, 'when the Taliban began enacting their plan to rebuild Afghanistan in their own liking, there was no place for Hazaras, or any minorities, within that. We began to hear whisperings, and then stories, of a campaign against our people: from land displacement to slaughters and executions.'

As the ideology of the Taliban, and the soldiers carrying that ideology, began to creep ever closer to Abbas's village, his family were left with a choice. With their community dwindling around them as other households began to flee, the Nazari family could either stay and await persecution, or they could flee as well. One day, Abbas's father told him that tomorrow would be his last day at school, and to say goodbye to his teachers, because they were leaving. His family packed all they could manage into duffel bags, climbed into the back of a truck, and moved forwards into the unknown.

The story from here is something I can't do justice to in a few hundred words, so I highly recommend reading Abbas's bestselling book, *After the Tampa*, to learn the full details of their incredible journey. Escaping across the border into Pakistan, the family then spent six desperate months relying on corruption, bribery, begging and pure luck to make it to Indonesia, where they spent what remained of their life savings to buy passage on an asylum boat headed for Australia. They were promised a two-day journey on a sturdy, seaworthy vessel. Instead, when they went to board, they were presented with the *Palapa II* — a rickety old wooden fishing boat, designed for a crew of forty — crammed with 438 men, women and children, including seven-year-old Abbas, all hoping for a better life. The situation was so dire that some families began to cry, refusing to board the unseaworthy vessel, and shouting in anger at the smugglers who had lied to them and taken their money. Abbas's father simply reassured his family: 'Have faith, we've made it this far.'

'When I look back on my story, I was just a child tagging along for a wild ride with my family. I was oblivious to the wider circumstances of our journey, which thankfully shielded me from the weight and trauma of it all. Children are naturally resilient and so I consider myself lucky to go through what we went through at the age that I did. Young enough to remember, but too young to understand.'

The journey was far from over. As the *Palapa* fought its way through the Indian Ocean and into the Pacific, on the first night the engine began to splutter, and then died. They were adrift in the middle of the ocean, in the middle of nowhere — with no radio, and no help on the way. As people desperately tried to repair the engine, and ripped wooden panels from the deck in a futile attempt to paddle the boat across an ocean, storm clouds began to gather. The passengers spent the night being thrown around in the storm, as vomit and luggage and bodies rolled around below deck, breaking bones, and praying they would make it through. 'Even as a child, it was pretty clear to me — I knew we were about to die.'

When the dawn broke, the *Palapa* was badly damaged and had taken on huge amounts of water, which passengers were trying to bail. But the dawn also brought hope, in the shape of a cargo ship on the horizon. It was a Norwegian vessel called the *Tampa*, which enacted one of the largest maritime rescues in modern history. All passengers were saved with only the clothes on their backs — the *Palapa* sank shortly after the rescue with the passengers' few belongings on board.

What followed became one of the most contentious political spats in Australian diplomatic history, after Australia refused to take the asylum seekers (in line with their obligations under international law) and instead told the *Tampa*'s captain to return them to Indonesia. The ensuing drama involved 48 fully armed Australian SAS soldiers, the asylum seekers being held on the sweltering deck of the *Tampa* in the middle of the ocean, and weeks of international diplomacy and negotiations. It's now known as the *Tampa* Affair. Eventually, New Zealand agreed to accept all of the family groups, totalling about 130 people, and Abbas reached New Zealand shores.

At this point, I have to pause to take it all in. I ask Abbas about how he looks back on this incredible adversity and what it taught him at the time. 'I have vivid memories of our journey, but what I lacked was the understanding, and the true weight of it all. It's only in hindsight that I have a greater understanding of the gravity and nature of the journey we were forced to take. Like all obstacles, you don't fully understand what you've learnt or why you went through those struggles until well after the dust has settled. And yes, if you find value in those lessons, then they do stick with you.'

Eventually, the family were resettled in Christchurch, where they began to build a new life, a new identity, a new sense of purpose and belonging — in a place that was very different to everything they had known. I couldn't imagine how hard this must have been. Abbas explained:

'In Sungjoy, we had all the things that make life worth living: identity, community, a sense of belonging, a deep connection to culture and the land. All of that was stripped away from us when we were forced to flee, and in New Zealand, it took many years to regain those things. Learning to rebuild a hyphenated identity and a place of belonging in a foreign land is a tough mission. But having the support of our new community in Upper Riccarton meant that transition was easy. Had we not had the support of our new community, my story would have been very different.'

Still, their family leaned into their father's words: 'Have faith, we've made it this far.'

As we chatted, I heard a lot about how Abbas learnt to thrive in this new country. But I figured there had to be so much more to the whole experience — the adversity of being uprooted and replanted on the other side of the world in an entirely unfamiliar place, of learning the language, learning to fit in, learning who you are at a time of life when so much already feels uncertain. Abbas told me that whilst all of that is true, it doesn't necessarily decide the outcome — in fact, with the right attitude, it can work the opposite way: 'What we tell ourselves has a profound impact on how we see ourselves and the world. If you constantly ruminate on how you've been victimised, or how the cards you've been dealt aren't ideal, then you'll generally take on a negative perspective on life. Rumination is powerful only if you focus on a positive lens. Victimhood can be crippling or empowering — you get to decide.'

Spurred on by that attitude, Abbas began to thrive within his new life fairly quickly, showing that natural resilience he referred to earlier. 'I loved my time at high school. Burnside High School is a larger school, meaning we had access to subjects and experiences that other schools didn't. I'd describe myself as an all-rounder — athletic enough to make the First XV and the Secondary Schools Athletics Champs, as well as being in the accelerated maths and science classes.

'The biggest thing I learnt from high school was that opportunity looks like hard work at first, which is why most people avoid it, but the rewards reveal themselves after. I've always been an optimist by nature, so I'd always look at the potential in something, as opposed to the work involved. For example, in year 9, my English teacher told me about the upcoming New Zealand Spelling Bee. I'd always been good at spelling, and thought I had a chance. I entered, and placed second in Canterbury and third at Nationals.' Not bad for a guy who five years earlier hadn't known a word of English!

Abbas eventually went on to study international relations at the University of Canterbury, before becoming a policy analyst at the New Zealand Treasury. He then received a Fulbright

Scholarship to attend Georgetown University in Washington DC where he graduated with a Master's in security studies. Now, Abbas owns and operates two successful gyms, has been a semi-finalist for Young New Zealander of the Year, is a bestselling author, and is only just getting started.

His whole family has likewise thrived in their new life on the other side of the world, with a few Master's degrees, a pilot's licence, a couple of scholarships to US colleges, and a successful family business between them. It's a stark contrast from their life in a far-flung region of a distant country, or the vulnerable stateless people crammed into a sinking ship in the middle of the ocean, or the disempowered pawns in an international political game. They kept faith, and now, they've made it 'this far'. I asked Abbas what, throughout this journey, gave him and his family the resilience to just keep moving forwards.

'One of the things which has stuck with me the whole way through my experiences is that things are never as bad as they seem when you're in it. Oftentimes, we are so stuck down in the weeds and the little day-to-day stuff that we forget to lift our heads to get a glance at the bigger picture. The little blips in the graph can seem like chasms when we are zoomed so far in. There's lots of relief when you zoom out and see the greater context.'

I asked him about keeping faith, as their father had always told them, and what it means to him. 'Faith and values are something that we often don't talk about in life, or don't actually know how to talk about. Having faith is the ability to listen to that voice, or in some cases, multiple voices, in your head. It doesn't mean heeding what they say, but being in tune with the feeling. It provides a guiding light in times of distress or confusion. You may not know the answer, or where the path is headed, but have faith.' For Abbas, that faith lies in his guiding values — a starting point to show him the next steps, even if the whole path might not be clear in the depths of adversity. Faith took their family into Pakistan, to Indonesia, in a boat across the ocean, and on to New Zealand — all the while that path ahead was impossible to see. It's a powerful guiding force.

'If I had a time machine, I wouldn't change anything, because without adversity there is no pathway to resilience. Resilience is not something that can be taught in a seminar or a book — it's built through experience. It's tough to appreciate it when you're going through the battles, but those scars are a testament to your learning.'

# 6

# STAND ALONGSIDE

In 2019, I had the opportunity to travel to the United States and lead three days of workshops on resilience for the US Forest Service. They're the people represented by Smokey Bear, the cartoon bear who says, 'Only *you* can prevent forest fires!' (Evidently a bear with more serious preoccupations than Winnie the Pooh.) Anyway, the US Forest Service had been through a few tough years, culminating in the massive California bushfires of 2018 which burnt about 800,000 hectares of land — an area twice the size of the whole Auckland region. One of their crucial roles is forest-fire prevention and preparation (see: talking bear), and as California scorched, then-President Donald Trump fired off a tweet blaming them for the destruction, then stated in a subsequent interview that it was the failure of the Forest Service to rake up dead leaves which led to so much damage being done.

I had the opportunity to work with some of their teams from all over the country the following year, and morale was understandably low. Mental health was a huge issue for these hard-working people — due to the nature of the job, many of their employees are stationed in extremely remote and isolated areas.

At the end of one of my presentations, I had a chat with a guy who was kitted out in wilderness gear — khaki pants and shirt, fleece vest and a canvas sunhat, despite a perfectly satisfactory conference-room ceiling overhead. He must've been about sixty or so, judging by his white beard. He looked the part of a true mountain man, a softly spoken, calm, wise and competent person who had lived through much and survived it all. As I stood there, I thought that if I were to stumble across a mountain lion or a bear, he was the person I would want by my side.

He thanked me for my presentation, then leaning in, in a drawl so slow that I was near bursting with anticipation, he gave me one of the most profound takes on resilience I've ever heard. What he said was: 'In the US Forest Service, we have two rules to ensure we don't die out there in the wilderness. We don't go out unprepared, and we don't climb mountains alone. I think you might find that applies to resilience and adversity as well.'

I felt he'd pretty much hit the nail on the head. How do we face life, and the adversity within it? First and foremost: not unprepared. Not only is this common sense, it's also the purpose of this book — each and every chapter is dedicated to that preparation, the stockpiling of tools and skills in preparation for adversity. But secondly, and the purpose of this chapter specifically: we don't climb mountains alone. The next S is Stand Alongside: the idea of leaning on and pulling in people who are close to us during times of adversity — even if this seems like the opposite of our natural inclination during tough times.

## Don't Climb Mountains Alone

When I talk to people about my cancer, and they ask me what helped me the most through that time and what gave me the resilience to keep going, the full answer is (not coincidentally) as thick as this book. So, to save both of us time, I give them the short answer, a core element of which is 'the support of the people around me: my family, including my girlfriend, my friends, and the nurses and other staff on the ward'. I feel this goes some way towards giving the credit which is so rightly due to these people for all they did for me while I was in hospital, both in terms of material and emotional support, and it's also absolutely the truth.

While I was on the ward, each of these people gave me many, many hours of company, sitting next to my hospital bed in the horrendous lime-green reclining chair that was in my room — the colour of which was so bad that when, only shortly after finding out that my very existence was in great jeopardy and I had months of horrific treatment ahead of me to try to save my life, it was not my situation but rather the chair for which the nurses apologised as they wheeled me into my new hospital room.

My girlfriend Jem, who was in the midst of studying and sitting her final exams, all while getting ready to move to Australia, and training for and competing in her athletics season, spent countless hours sitting by my bed. My mum and dad, my siblings, cousins, aunties and uncles, grandparents and others all spent innumerable hours by my side. Mates came in to be with me and cheer me up with their bad jokes. *People came to be with me.* They didn't even necessarily *do* anything, because there wasn't anything to be done — they were just *there*. Many expressions of support are based upon the idea of being physically present: 'showing up' for someone, or 'being there' for them. I felt, and was, supported just by people being around me.

Perhaps most notable of all, and something I didn't expect, was the personal support the nurses offered me. Many of them were young — only a few years older than me at the time — so we really clicked. When they weren't completely rushed off their feet, they would often come and sit with me and talk, mostly about life outside of this awful place (who they were without scrubs, who I was without a gown and with hair).

The connections that I made with these nurses was something I haven't encountered before or since. During my treatment, my entire life rested in their hands — any needs I had went through them, my connection to the outside world flowed through them. It's not just what they do, however — it's *how* they do it. They are the most kind, caring, selfless people I have ever met. They were humble, had a sense of humour and were able to take serious and uncomfortable situations and make them bearable. They came and talked to me so I didn't have to stare at the ceiling alone. They made an effort to get to know my family and me as real people. *They saved my life.*

•••••••••

The last few lines above are an excerpt from a speech I have delivered quite a few times to conferences for medical professionals over recent years, and to be honest, a few times now I've said them with tears streaming down my face. That is how much those people, and what they did for me, means to me.

Without their support, and that of my family and friends, I don't think I would have made it through my cancer. This is why it is so important to draw people close and lean on them during times of adversity — to *not climb that mountain alone*. Whatever adversity you're facing, big or small, you need to have people around you.

I've interviewed a few people about this topic, and they have their own stories about how this has applied in their own lives. All Black Will Jordan spoke about the importance of having a strong support network:

> 'I've been really lucky to have a really close family, and to just be able to be understood and listened to. It's knowing who you can talk to, but also knowing when to listen to them. Often just going to speak to someone can be quite difficult — [when I was younger] I don't know if I thought it was going to be awkward, I just didn't even know how to approach it.
>
> 'It's also one thing to talk to someone who is empathetic and understands your current problems, but another thing to talk to someone who is actually in your shoes and has been in the same scenario. I think in the high-performance world, we're a bit lucky in that you have so many people around you who have been in that same position, who have the same experiences,

> who share those trials and tribulations together — I think that's a big one.'

Chlöe Swarbrick also agreed that, in her work, it's essential to have a team on your side:

> 'The most important thing for anybody who is interested in changing how things operate — but also finding a semblance of resilience — is to find something bigger than yourself and to play a part or a role in that. Because that is the community that will hold you when things don't go particularly well.'

And just to really make the point, Olympian Zoe Hobbs credits finding the right support team as a key factor in her success:

> 'I think a big part of it is just having an incredible team behind me who I have a lot of confidence and trust in. They back me, they have a lot of confidence in me to achieve what they know I can achieve. And so, through them, I gain a lot of confidence.'

As well as these stories of personal experience, scientific research shows that people who draw on the support of those around them are more resilient when faced with adversity. The opposite is also true: people who are socially withdrawn don't do as well. While all of the Four Ss are backed up by research, Standing Alongside is perhaps the one with the greatest weight and body of proof behind it. We know for a fact that people who climb mountains alone, who go through tough times in isolation, have shockingly bad outcomes compared to people who have a community to support them, who belong to something bigger than themselves. Human beings are hard-wired to be social, and there's something so powerfully negative about loneliness and isolation that it seems to break even the most resilient people.

You may have seen this yourself, at a huge societal level, in the course of your life already. In the aftermath of a natural disaster or a shared community adversity, perhaps the most palpable sense is one of pulling together and unifying. For instance, my greatest recollection of the Christchurch earthquakes, when I was thirteen, is of the incredibly powerful sense of unity, connection and belonging that we felt in the days and weeks following — we were all suffering, and we were suffering together, and we all had each other's backs through that suffering. Likewise, I experienced the same sensation when I worked in Kaikōura to deliver content around resilience after the devastating earthquakes there in 2016. Maybe you felt this after the 2019 mosque shootings in Christchurch, or when Cyclone Gabrielle hit the North Island in 2023 — when things are falling apart, people are drawn to each other, for support and to support one another. When times are tough, we feel connected. Studies done across the globe, on a wide range of different cultures and countries, have consistently shown the extraordinarily powerful impact that this bonding and collective identity can have in terms of buffering against mental-health impacts, reducing isolation, and enabling both individual and collective resilience. Basically, we pull together when times are tough because it works. We are safe when we feel like we belong.

Hopefully, there are many places where you feel you belong. If you're at school, hopefully your class feels welcoming. Hopefully, you feel you belong in a family and a friend group. Maybe you feel you belong in a sports team, a cultural or arts pursuit, a religion. Whatever it is for you, I can tell you that, based on scientific research, it's incredibly important that you seek out a place to belong and continue to invest in building it.

Unfortunately, often during our lowest points we can tend to pull away from those around us. We might feel like we need to hide or shy away, or feel like others don't understand us, or don't want to. Maybe we feel ashamed or embarrassed about what is going on for us and how we are reacting, or as if this is something we need to face alone. We shrivel up, draw further and further into ourselves, hide what is going on inside. When we need people the most, we're at our most likely to push them away, even subconsciously and without realising.

This type of withdrawal or pushing people away happens often when someone is suffering from significant mental distress, such as anxiety or depression. Unfortunately, there can still be social stigma around these conditions, so when adversity escalates into a mental-health issue, people sometimes work even harder to hide what's going on with them. Because of this, someone who is already suffering can end up being even more isolated.

Let me state this categorically, specifically in the context of mental illness: *you need to know that you can't fight this one alone. You need to open up and ask for help.*

You might think you can outrun it — and maybe you can for a while. You can numb it, but that's no long-term fix. The only way out is to ask for help.

And if you are on the other side of the coin, watching someone you care about resisting reaching out for help, be there for them, even if they try to minimise their situation or push you away. Keep an eye out for warning signs: changes in their thought patterns (more self-criticism, trouble concentrating), changes in their feelings (excessive gloom, worry, guilt, fear, sadness, anger, helplessness, hopelessness or loneliness), changes in their behaviour (overreacting to situations, changes in school performance, wild changes in their goals or motivations, a sense of 'I don't recognise this person anymore'), or unexpected physical changes (in weight, appearance, sleep and energy levels).

But more than any of these magic 'signs' being the key to knowing something is wrong, you'll often just have a feeling — and that shouldn't be ignored. Without diminishing its importance, it's not actually that hard to do: if you have an inkling that something might be wrong, ask them in private, 'Hey mate, is everything okay? You seem out of sorts lately.' You have absolutely nothing to lose — the worst that can happen, if you take them aside and privately ask how they're going, is that they laugh and tell you they're fine, and they come away knowing you care about them.

I don't take this stuff lightly, because I've seen it play out — and sadly, maybe you have, too. I had other friends who I wanted to interview for this book, to share their perspectives, but I couldn't because they aren't here anymore. Incredible young people who had achieved so much in such a short time, but who never progressed any further because they were picked off by mental illness. Individually, and as a society, we are being robbed of so much potential when we don't protect those who need our help.

Whether the context is mental distress, or cancer, or feeling stressed about an upcoming exam, the answer is *always* to draw people in close. It doesn't have to be forced or awkward (as I was so concerned about when I was at high school). It's as straightforward as keeping people updated on what is going on in your life, both the good and the bad, honestly and completely.

It's so natural to want to only share the good with people, maybe out of a fear of burdening them with your struggles or being embarrassed about how you feel, but it's just as important to have a core group of people around you who you can share the bad with.

By sharing your own disasters as well as your triumphs, you encourage and demonstrate to those around you that it's okay for them to do the same.

I've talked about the powerful relationships I had with the nurses, because those relationships were built on the trust I had to place in them to look after me and care for me at the very lowest, most vulnerable, most fragile time of my life. You might also remember that in chapter 4 'Salvage', I talked about how vulnerability creates trust, and trust creates connection. This doesn't just apply to hospital staff, but to all relationships. Your parents and family have seen you at your very lowest points and still love you. Likewise, the bond you have with your closest friends or partner is so strong because you share everything with them, your hopes and dreams for the future, your good as well as your bad. They know secrets of yours that no one else does.

To create these deep connections, you have to make yourself

vulnerable. For this reason alone, you should never fear reaching out or sharing the adversity you are facing and the impact it's having on you — it's a pathway to a deeper and greater connection with the people you lean on and who lean on you.

So it's a win-win, right? During times of adversity, leaning on people both bolsters your resilience, and further develops your support network for the future.

Particularly as you get older, your mates will be a huge part of your support network — the people you will lean on during adversity. They, in turn, will do the same to you. In many ways, you will know them better than even their parents do — you will know more of the details of their life, the adversities they are facing, the pressures they are under. They'll probably be more willing to talk to you than to their parents, too. So if anyone is in a position to support them, or be there for them to lean on during the tough times, it's you.

This transition, where your support network begins to expand, is in many ways something which defines the shift from being a child to becoming an adult. As a child, your entire support network comprises your caregivers and your wider family. As an adult, that network expands to be far, far broader — encompassing mates, colleagues, romantic partners, new people you encounter along the way — and there comes a time when your parents and family form a far smaller piece of this support network than they did previously, until one day, you'll find yourself looking after your parents, not the other way around.

Because of this, one really important part of making this transition from child to adult is to begin to build these networks and connections, to ensure that as you move out into the world, you have that support around you.

## Pick Your Team

Talking about mates leads me on to something else which is absolutely critical to how successful and happy you will become in your life: carefully choosing the people you surround yourself with.

About 2000 years ago, a Greek philosopher called Epictetus wrote: 'The key is to keep company only with people who uplift you, whose presence calls forth your best.' It must have been a solid bit of advice because it has not lost any truth in the last two millennia.

You will have heard it all before, no doubt. You might have heard the quotes 'You are the sum of the five people you spend the most time with', or 'Show me your friends and I'll show you your future'. Your parents might have lectured you about not falling in with 'the wrong crowd'. If you've got into trouble once or twice, a solemn-faced teacher might have told you that you can do better than associating with those 'troublemakers' who will drag you down. The thing is, as much as you hate hearing it, it's completely true.

I have a fairly tight-knit group of friends. I have a wider circle beyond that, of people who I enjoy spending time with and value, but in terms of my core group, there are just a few. But all of them have something in common: *they are better people than me.*

At the absolute minimum, I think that they are better than me at a major component of life, and for that reason I aspire to be more like them and learn from them. The thing they're good at is not necessarily anything tangible, like being great at swimming or cracking jokes; it's more based on their values. For instance, I admire their persistence and dedication, or their bravery and courage, or their kindness and compassion for others.

Without being too much of a suck-up, I'm truly in awe of the people I'm closest to. I learn a huge amount from them and take away a huge amount of inspiration. I am a better person for being around them. I think I naturally gravitate towards these people because they are strong where I am weak, and I want to learn and absorb as much as possible from them.

I have friends who accomplish extraordinary physical feats far beyond what I'm yet capable of, friends who are brighter than I'll ever be who focus on areas of study I don't know the first thing about, friends who have deeper and more meaningful perspectives on life which I want to learn. Friends who value completely different things to me, friends who challenge my own thoughts and beliefs, friends who are good people and support me.

I think this is how it ought to be: you should look at the people you choose to have around you and go, 'Wow, I really look up to and admire these people!' Why else would you choose them to be your friends?

When you consider the people you choose to surround yourself with, think about each of these four questions. Hopefully the answer is yes:

1. Am I inspired to learn from them, because they are better than me in some way?
2. Do I admire them for who they are as a person (not just for their achievements and accomplishments)?
3. Do they bring out the best in me, and does being around them make me a better person?
4. Better yet, do they *encourage* me to be a better person, and want me to improve?

There's plenty more to friendships: we get along, we've got common interests, being with them makes me feel good, they are loyal and trustworthy, and so on. But I think you should put conscious effort and awareness into the bigger questions, too, because they're not necessarily what you think of when you first make friends — but they can make a critical difference to your life.

Even beyond the idea that the people you surround yourself with will make you a better person, their impact on your life and wellbeing overall is huge. The people you surround yourself with will influence not only what you learn and therefore your abilities, but also your opinions and beliefs, your dreams and aspirations, your decisions and actions, your attitudes and emotions — and this can be scientifically proven. A study released in 2008 which had followed participants over a period of twenty years concluded that *people's happiness was determined largely by the happiness of those around them*, and vice versa, to quite an astounding extent.

Happy people positively impact the people around them for up to three degrees of separation — in other words, the impact of you being happy and positive in everyday life can be reliably measured in your friend's friend's friend, if that makes any sense. On the other side of the equation, if you surround yourself with negative people, you're negatively impacting not only your own wellbeing, but that of your parents and everyone around them as well. You mightn't be able to see it yourself, but you truly are a creation of the people you choose to be around — for better or worse. For that reason it's worth being pretty selective about who they are.

## Summary

- To give yourself the resilience to get through tough times, it's important to lean on and share your feelings with those closest to you. Make a conscious effort to do so, for two reasons:
    1. If you're not consciously or intentionally pulling people closer during adversity, you're probably unconsciously pushing them away; and
    2. Even your close friends and family can be so tied up with their own busy lives that they aren't just ready and waiting to reach out to you or recognise the adversity you're experiencing. This doesn't mean they don't care; it just means you need to make an effort to share it with them.
- Sometimes people will reach out to you to check if you're doing okay, or because you seem out of sorts to them. If they do offer you help or even just a chat, don't

reject it — from the outside, they may have a better or certainly different perspective on what you're feeling inside. I know I've been in this position before — and when I've been willing to talk with people about things that are bothering me, I've almost always come away feeling better for it.

- To be supported by, and to support, others is a huge part of life in the real world. In some ways, that transition from childhood to adulthood is largely defined by the time where you begin to lean on a broader support network than just your family. To capture that benefit, though, you have to be ready and willing to open up and share, as difficult as you may (or may not) find it.
- Find good people to surround yourself with. Learn from them and aspire to be like them in ways in which they are strong and you are weak. Monitor the impact they have on you — do they push you towards your values and goals?
- When things get tough, lean on those people — tell them the truth about what is going on for you, and how it feels. Don't only share your hopes and dreams and successes — share your fears and losses and regrets. Don't fall victim to the common mistake of closing up and hiding the ugly parts — you can be the most resilient person walking the planet, but you still can't expect to carry it all alone.
- Expect to be there in return for them in their time of need. Watch over them, and if you sense something is up, ask the question.
- Don't climb mountains alone. We all need a climbing partner.

## Chlöe Swarbrick — Stronger Together

Chlöe Swarbrick is the co-leader of the Green Party of Aotearoa New Zealand, Member of Parliament (MP) for Auckland Central, a former mayoral candidate for Auckland and, I hate to say it, young. I hate to say it because I know for a fact she's sick of hearing it: when we sat down to chat for this book, one of the first stories she told me was about a mayoral debate in which the moderator referred to her (aged twenty-two at the time) as the youngest candidate, and she immediately asked why no one found it interesting that sitting mayor Phil Goff was the oldest candidate — a response which Phil apparently didn't love!

Chlöe first entered Parliament aged twenty-three as a list MP for the Greens. At the time, she was the youngest MP in forty-two years, and again, she was not allowed to forget it: 'I've been told live on national radio that I'm too young and therefore have no idea what I'm talking about. Even if I can refer to the facts and the evidence and research, sometimes people *still* don't want to engage with me.'

That's their prerogative, Chlöe says, and she obviously doesn't let other people's opinions hold her back.

'It's just trying to constantly reframe that and talk to people whose opinions you really value. I've got a core group of people I'll often touch base with when I feel a little bit unmoored, people who've been through similar experiences who I've accumulated over time, and friends who have known me since before this oddity befell me.

'I have had the worst things imaginable said to me through my email and my DMs on social media, and I think it's important to be 110 per cent honest about this: it sometimes really gets to me. In those times, having people around me is really important.'

Starting at the beginning, I asked what set her on the path to becoming one of New Zealand's most well-known politicians.

'My time at high school, completely openly, was very challenging. I was coming to grips with mental ill-health and what that meant,' she replied. 'I was also playing around with the idea of what it meant to go from being traditionally academically successful to being quite bored with that, and trying to push boundaries — because of stuff that was happening in my personal life, but also because of feeling rebellious about who I was in relation to the rest of the world, feeling angry at the injustices . . . all of those things [that] I think come with the tumult of growing up. It ended up getting all very overwhelming and challenging, and I decided that I probably had to leave — I had to leave home, and I had to leave high school, and not do year 13.'

I asked Chlöe about what gave her the resilience to get through those times, and her answer reminded me of the importance of learning these skills sooner rather than later: 'At that point in time, I hadn't developed those strategies which I learnt later on — and I wish I had developed them earlier. It's only as I've got older that I've found that language to reach out and ask for help.'

After several years taking a whole range of different opportunities — including starting and running a number of business and community projects, working as a journalist, and completing a Bachelor of Arts and a Bachelor of Laws — Chlöe decided to run for the Auckland mayoralty. Her work as a journalist kickstarted the idea, after she interviewed a range of 'uninspiring' candidates and became disillusioned by how disconnected many of them were from the issues facing young people.

Chlöe's campaign, run with no political experience and next to no budget, was ultimately unsuccessful, although she polled third overall (out of nineteen candidates) with 29,000 votes, and gained a whole lot of recognition and admiration. This set her on the path to national-level politics, becoming a candidate for the Green Party and entering Parliament at the next election.

Six years later, Chloë is co-leader of the Greens and MP for Auckland Central, and I ask her how she manages to cope with the public scrutiny and criticism of being the youngest leader of a political party in the country.

'I see resilience not so much as the individual trait that it's so often lauded as — I see it instead as being part of something bigger than yourself which can hold you when you need that time and space, because it's otherwise completely unsustainable. I don't think anybody can know who they are without understanding who they are in the context of community.'

I was particularly interested in how Chlöe deals with the abuse which comes about as part of her work. As Chlöe noted, being involved in meaningful work and fighting hard for things which matter to you often means having to face criticism and judgement. Maintaining a sense of belonging and connection and the support of friends are vital to her, as are being true to her core values and sense of overall purpose.

'Another thing which keeps me resilient in the space of politics — which is quite disorienting and where the things which I care about are constantly challenged and tested — is to know that the most important thing is the change you're fighting for, and that I would sacrifice my perceived career or hierarchical status for that purpose. That is what keeps me sane and grounded in that space — knowing that I'm there for the pursuit of change, rather than the pursuit of personal status or glory.'

Here's one final thing Chlöe said which stuck with me: 'We have this tendency to attribute progress to one person. Whether it be Martin Luther King Jr and the civil rights movement, or Kate Sheppard and the suffragette movement, we find the one person who gave the really good speeches with the sickest quotes, and we pin it on them.

'But if you stop and think about it, those people would be marching down empty streets or speaking to empty rooms if it weren't for the collective who joined and supported them. So I guess the biggest thing I've come to realise about resilience is that finding your people and how you can contribute is the most powerful thing you can do — because no one sustainably changes the world all on their own, despite what we sometimes like to think.

'Change, particularly on the scale which is necessary to meet things like the crisis of inequality or the climate crisis, is simply not going to be an individual, one-person feat.'

# 7

# VALUES: IDENTIFY WHAT MATTERS TO YOU

When I speak at schools about values, I always start with a deliberately exaggerated: 'Hands up who is excited for me to talk about values?!' I do this for my own entertainment, because without fail, I get about two hands: one person who is taking the piss, and someone else who feels sorry for me because they know no one else is going to put their hand up. The rest of the audience slips down in their seats, and I'm not at all surprised.

As a society, we've pretty much killed the concept of 'values'. We've taken something which, in terms of psychology, is fascinating and integral to our resilience, success and wellbeing, and turned it into something both contentious and boring at the same time.

When we look at values through a positive lens, we tend to put them up as something to be aspired towards: a list of actions or behaviours to strive for. That is the context you will be most familiar with — like school or sports club values, or your parents telling you something you *must* do, a way you *must* behave. There's very little — if any — discussion of the real-life impacts of values: instead, it's just a list of rules or expectations placed upon you.

Then, when people fail to live up to these 'values', we immediately pile on and attack. Values and morals seem to be the first thing that people jump to when there's a failure or shortcoming of a person or an organisation — we question their values, or say they don't align with ours. They are what we attack during political debates. They've become a big stick which we wield, coming at values from a place of deficit or failure, rather than anything positive, let alone useful.

Basically, society has made values into a set of rules, then when people don't follow those rules, we use values to bash them. Values are simultaneously a measuring stick and a whacking stick — we use them to see if people measure up, or we use them to cut other people down. Hardly a surprise that no one finds them exciting, right?

........

So, if values aren't a list of rules, or a tool to judge people by, then what actually are they? *Values decide how we live our life and make our decisions*. They dictate your response to everything that happens to you, without you even having to think about it. In terms of resilience, values are how we survive or how we don't survive. They are how you keep going, or how you fall short.

If that all sounds a bit deep, the best explanation of values I've ever heard is that values are the things you will get into a fight over. What are the things on which you will stand your ground? What are the things which piss you off when other people do, or don't do, them? What do you believe in? Those things are either a value for you, or you have an underlying value which drives that belief.

Can't stand discrimination? You probably have strong values of fairness and equality. Hate cheats? You probably value justice and honesty. Cringe when other people don't have good manners? You have a strong value of gratitude. Hopefully you can start to see values not as a set of rules, not as the absence of mistakes, but instead as *integral parts of what makes you up*.

> Values are you. You are your values.

I can't stress enough how significant this is, but the science can. Psychologists have worked really hard, for decades, to try to find what factors result in high levels of human wellbeing — the idea being that if we could find a common factor that makes people happy, regardless of occupation, race, age, gender or how much money they have, then we could not only identify people who need help earlier, but we should also be able to *add happiness* to people's lives by encouraging that thing. For instance, if you did a big study and found out that people who drink their coffee *before* they eat their breakfast are happier than the people who have breakfast before coffee, across all ages, races, countries, wealth and income levels, then we may have found the underlying key to happiness.

Unfortunately, it's not that. Psychologists have tested just about every variable you can imagine, whether that's income levels, family size, where you live, intelligence, diet, ethnic background, amount of free time or political opinions. There is one factor which they have found most accurately predicts wellbeing and how happy someone is in life.

Can you guess what it is? I know from asking a wide range of audiences this question that it's probably not what you're thinking. It's not 'How much do you earn?', or 'How many people do you have in your support network', or 'Do you live in a first- or third-world country?', or even 'Is the glass half full or half empty?' The question is:

Do you live your life in accordance with your values?

That's it. In other words, 'Does the way you live your life line up with the things you really, deeply believe in and value?' It really is that simple. If people can honestly answer yes, research has proven that they are more likely to enjoy a higher level of wellbeing. If they answer no, it's lower. This question has proved to be the most accurate indicator of wellbeing so far.

••••••••

It's not hard to see why values dictate your wellbeing, given that they are a major part of what creates meaning in our lives. If we don't feel our lives have meaning, we are not as happy as we could be. For example, if your values centre around *connectedness*, *relationships* and *popularity* and you end up working as a parking warden, chances are your level of wellbeing is not going to be very high, because your values won't be being met. On the other hand, if your values set is around *accountability*, *fairness* and *justice*, then you'll probably be quite happy in your life as a parking warden, but not necessarily in some other role.

This is why recognising your values and having what is important to you clear in your mind is so critical, particularly when you are a teenager, because this will hopefully make it easier for you to choose your pathway. These values are the things which you should be falling back on and considering when you begin to think about your future and the opportunities you want to pursue.

For me, some of my values are around *connectedness*, *people* and *impact*, and as a result I'm incredibly happy doing this work. As I said earlier, before my cancer I thought I wanted to work in the fields of law or commerce. While it's certainly possible that I would've found a role in those areas which fulfilled my values, there are some other careers that fit in well with them, such as teaching. My story and how I ended up doing the work I do now is a really good example of this — my work now hasn't just come about because of the things I learnt during cancer, but rather as a direct result of my values. Even after my experiences, if my values were in a different space — say *accountability*, *fairness* and *justice* instead — I would probably be doing something completely different, because this work wouldn't have fulfilled those values. I do this not just because I've been lucky to get the opportunity, but because it also happens to *align with what is important to me.*

.........

So, my first point in terms of why values matter is that the science tells us that *they are incredibly important to our overall wellbeing and in dictating our future*, by enabling us to play to our strengths when we choose our path forward. Then there's also the resilience side of things.

Taking my story as an example, facing cancer is one of those rare experiences in life when situations are so highly charged and every decision so consequential, yet so unfamiliar, that values almost become tangible objects guiding you through your lowest points. There's no guide for what to do next, how to act, how to feel — and this can be true during all forms of adversity. When you feel like you have no idea what to do when faced with adversity, it's your values which will guide you.

The necessity of some values and traits became abundantly apparent during my time facing cancer. These are the ones that helped me get through treatment, and without them I don't know if I would have made it: *grit*, *courage* and *persistence*. Others have become part of the lasting changes within me — the things that cancer has taught me: values such as *gratitude* and *perspective*. This is the second reason why values matter: they dictate how you will respond and react during the toughest points of your life.

.........

It's really important to note that *all values are good* — they universally have the ability to be your strengths. *None are better than others*. Actually, if you do view some values as better than others, that is very telling, because it gives you an indication of what is important to you.

Different things are important to different people. No two people are exactly alike, because we all value slightly different things. It's also why you get on better with some people than with others, and why you might fall in love with one person and not another — because your values are in alignment. Having different values to someone doesn't make you any better or worse than them, it just explains why some people seem to be 'on the same page' and others are not.

So, how do you figure out what your core values are — the things that are really important to you? Well, on the next page is a list of 154 values. Read through them — all of them — and I guarantee that some will jump out at you. Some will connect with you, and catch your attention or evoke a feeling inside you more than others. If this is your book, then grab a pen and chuck a circle around those ones which catch your eye — there might be as many as fifteen or twenty of them. If it's not your book, and you're not all that keen to get a whacking from a librarian, then make a list on paper or on your phone of the ones which catch your eye.

You might see aspects of many of these values in yourself. Many of them will be traits which you aspire to, or you can think of examples of how you exhibit them. It's just that some of them will be *more important* to you than others. This is the magic of values — they are all important, they are all strengths, they all mean something to us, and we strive towards all of them, but some will mean more to you than others. *Those are your personal values.* Don't fall into the trap of wanting to circle all of them because they're all important, or all admirable, or you want your life to reflect every one of them — pay attention to which ones speak really strongly to you.

This is also far from an exhaustive list — if there are other values or ideas which you connect with, feel free to add them as well.

---

## Values List

acceptance
accountability
achievement
adaptability
adventure
advocacy
altruism
ambition
appreciation
authenticity
balance
beauty
being the best
belonging
boldness
brilliance
calmness
career
caring
challenge
charity
cheerfulness
collaboration
commitment
community
compassion
competence
confidence
connection
consistency
contentment
contribution
cooperation
courage
creativity
credibility
curiosity
daring
decisiveness
dedication
dependability
dignity

diversity
efficiency
empathy
encouragement
engagement
enthusiasm
environment
equality
ethics
excellence
expressiveness
fairness
faith
family
flexibility
forgiveness
freedom
friendships
fun
future generations
generosity
giving back
grace
gratitude
growth
happiness
harmony
health
home
honesty
hope
humility
humour
inclusion
independence
individuality
initiative
innovation
inspiring others
integrity
intelligence
intuition
joy
justice
kindness
knowledge
leadership
learning
legacy
leisure
love
loyalty
making a difference
mindfulness
motivation
nature
open-mindedness
optimism
originality
passion
patience
peace
perfection
performance
perseverance
playfulness
popularity
power
preparedness
pride
punctuality
recognition
relationships
reliability
resilience
resourcefulness
respect
responsibility
risk-taking
safety
security
self-control
selflessness
self-respect

serenity
service
simplicity
spirituality
sportsmanship
stability
stewardship
success
teamwork
thankfulness
thoughtfulness
time
tradition
travel
trust
truth
understanding
uniqueness
usefulness
versatility
vision
vulnerability
warmth
wealth
wellbeing
wholeheartedness
wisdom
zeal

---

I've always felt sharing your personal values with other people is a bit like sharing your Spotify Wrapped on your story at the end of the year — as in, everyone's got one, and no one cares about yours. But for the sake of the exercise, some of the values which jump out for me are *health*, *happiness*, *optimism*, *connectedness*, *loyalty*, *achievement*, *freedom*, *resilience*, *making a difference*, *family*, *leadership*, *gratitude*, *zeal* and *growth*. Yours are likely to be completely different to mine — maybe you value *individuality* or *forgiveness* or *creativity*. Some of yours might be the same as mine, but the odds that our lists are exactly the same are impossibly small — if I valued *listening* more highly, and had applied that in maths class, I would've been able to tell you the precise odds of you picking the exact same fifteen values as me, but I once had a maths teacher sit in on one of these presentations and, from what I recall, the odds were 0.0000000000000000003 per cent. For some perspective, to win the biggest Lotto prize in New Zealand, you need to select the winning six numbers out of forty. To get fifteen of the same values from a list of 154 is not happening. I'm confident enough about this that when I run the activity with a group, I usually offer up the rental car I've arrived in that day as a bet — if there's someone in the audience with those exact same values as mine, the car is all theirs. I'm not really sure how that would work legally, especially since half the time they don't even have a licence, but having run this exercise with thousands of people now, I've never had someone in the room share more than eight in common with me.

In a material sense, that is *one of the reasons why no two people are exactly alike* — because we all value slightly different things, which shape our attitudes and behaviours in different ways. It's also why you get on better or worse with some people than with others, and why you might fall in love with one person and not with someone else — because your values are more or less in alignment. Having different values doesn't make you any better or worse than anyone else, it just explains why you feel like some people are on the same page as you and others are not.

You might have a handful of values in common with your friends, maybe a few more in common with a partner or with your family members. You'll be lucky to ever meet someone who shares more than ten in common with you, to ever be in the same country as someone who shares twelve, and to ever walk on the planet with someone who has the exact same list as you.

........

Anyway, you should now have fifteen or so values in front of you — a list of the values which matter to you most. It's fine if you have a few more than that, but it will just mean this next step is going to be slightly more challenging.

Take your list, and rank the top five of those values *in order*. If you find it easier, you can rank all of your list and then select the top five, but either way you need to end up with a top five, ranked in order of importance. You're going to need to be a bit brutal and really look at your list to decide which ones are most important to you. Ask yourself:

> Which ones would you be you willing to compromise in pursuit of the others — and which ones are non-negotiable?

Taking my values, for example, I would have to ask myself whether *family* comes first, or if that value would be sidelined in order for me to follow my ambition of *making a difference*. Would I be willing to sacrifice *health* in order to chase *achievement*. Whether *happiness* means more to me than *loyalty*, or vice versa. By weighing up your list this way, you will find some values will naturally rise up and others will drop down a little. This might seem like an unnatural way to think, but it's not — we weigh up and prioritise our values in this way hundreds of times every day, like when your mate rocks up with a new haircut and asks if you like it, and you choose in the moment if you prioritise 'honesty' or 'kindness'.

Take your time on this and give it some serious thought. I'm regularly surprised by how long most people take when I run this as an exercise — ten to twenty minutes — and I'm glad they do, because it shows they are really thinking about it. These are not easy questions to answer. Hopefully, after a little time, you'll have a list of the five values which matter to you most, in order. These are the core elements of who you are, what makes you up as a person, why you think and act and interact with others the way you do.

As well as everyone's top values being different, every time I run this exercise I find almost everyone in the room has a different number-one value. Sharing these demonstrates just how unique we all are, and it's also a great way to learn a lot about your friends and classmates. What they choose says a lot about them as a person.

When I'm doing this exercise with young people, I also enjoy challenging them to think about *why* this is their most important value, or where that value comes from. Some research tells us that our values are mostly ingrained and set when we are really young — around seven years old — so they tend to come from or be influenced by the people we have spent the most time with by this age, such as our parents or families, or the experiences we've had in these years.

You might be able to see whether your values are directly influenced or indirectly shaped by those around you. Do your values align with your parents' values? If not, can you see how their values have shaped yours, even if that means forcing you off in another direction?

More than once I've had students list *freedom* or *independence* as their top value, because they feel that their families have been overbearing and controlling. I've had kids who list *risk-taking* as their top value, and found out that both their parents are entrepreneurs. Kids from challenging backgrounds often list *safety* or *stability* as being the most important.

No matter what the value or the reason, after doing this exercise students almost always feel like they've come away with a better understanding of themselves, and a bit of a gauge on why they do what they do and why they are the person they are. I hope you find it helpful, too.

.........

The final piece of the puzzle, and probably the most abstract, is to move from thinking about how your values influence your day-to-day actions, to focusing on how you can shift your day-to-day actions to be more in alignment with your values. It comes back to that wellbeing-predictor question we asked earlier:

> Do you live your life in accordance with your values?

This doesn't have to be a sit-down-and-write-a-list kind of activity — it's just something to think about. Clearly knowing your values and what matters to you will give you another point of reference to draw on during times of decision-making, whether that's choosing whether to go out with someone or what you want to do for a job or what to prioritise in life. You don't have to assess your whole life right now against these values — in fact, there probably isn't a great deal of benefit in you doing so. Your life as a young person is often largely not of your own making, so it's not particularly relevant whether you've set it up in alignment with your own values: you probably go to your school because it was chosen for you or because it's the local school. You hang out with the people there because they are the people there. You do what you're told to because, to a large extent, you're told to. Perhaps a better question is not 'Do you live your life in accordance with your values right now?', but rather, in two or five or ten years' time, when your life will be entirely of your own making, what would a life in accordance with those values look like? What job would it entail, who would your partner be, where would you live, what would you do with your spare time? It's important to carry these values in the back of your mind as you go about things, to help guide and shape that path.

This is most important during times of adversity. Like I said before, when things go wrong, there's usually no guide on how best to keep moving forward and how to get through in terms of your day-to-day actions. This is when your individual values become the most precious resource you have in terms of making decisions. These are the things you will draw in close and lean on to find your way through tough times, to remain resilient in the face of adversity.

I don't expect this chapter to change your expectations about what you want to do with the rest of your life. Like I said before, my values would fit well with my going into teaching, but I'm not really interested in doing that. Learning about my values when I was sixteen probably wouldn't have changed my plans in that respect, but what it would have done is made it clear in my mind that within the field I wanted to go into (law or commerce), I needed to work towards a role that would have fulfilled those needs. Otherwise, I would never have stuck with my job, because I wouldn't have found it fulfilling in the long term.

It's not about completely turning your whole life upside down right now and re-evaluating what you want to do. Even if learning this stuff about yourself doesn't revolutionise the way you want to move forward in life and what you want to do for a career, you can still use it to guide you in other small but significant ways.

## Summary

- Values are what make us who we are — they create the entirety of what we think, how we feel, how we live our lives and the decisions we make.
- Because of this, if you live your life in accordance with your values, you are exceptionally likely to have a high level of wellbeing — and if you don't, then you're almost certain to have a really poor level of wellbeing. A life in alignment with your values isn't just a bonus or 'nice to have' — it's what will dictate how good your time on this planet will be to a tremendous extent.
- Different things are important to different people, and all values are equally valid and important. No values are more or less important than others, although your perspective on that tells you much about yourself. Our

values make us unique as individuals, and they are quite literally why we are different to other people.

- Your list of values, particularly the top five, will be largely fixed for the rest of your life. If you've done this exercise properly, you can now take this information forward and use it to guide you reliably into the future — especially during periods of adversity.

## Jehan Casinader — Writing Your Own Story

Jehan Casinader is a journalist, public speaker and mental-health advocate. I first met Jehan when he interviewed me for a piece for *Seven Sharp* in 2016. At the time, he was twenty-six — and not only one of the most successful and high-profile reporters on television, but also one of the youngest. Given his age, you could be forgiven for thinking this must've been early in his career — in fact, his audacity as a teen had put him on screens across the country a whole heap earlier than that.

'I was a total nerd as a kid — I used to love watching the news each night. Apparently I was four years old when I told my parents I wanted to be a reporter.

'When I was thirteen, I was pretty confident, ambitious — and naïve. I decided to contact the biggest current affairs show in the country, *Holmes*, which aired right after the evening news. I asked them to let me do a story about the final *Lord of the Rings* movie, which had just premiered. They were crazy enough to give me a camera crew. That night, I remember sitting on the carpet at home, watching myself on TV, along with half a million other Kiwis. I was totally hooked.

'That made me even more confident' — at this point in our chat, I was struggling to imagine how this might be humanly possible — 'and I started contacting the editors at the *Herald* and *Sunday Star-Times*, claiming to be a freelance journalist. They didn't ask me for a CV or references. They didn't even ask if I'd been to journalism school. Instead, they started commissioning these massive feature articles that would end up in the papers on the weekend. Most of the editors had no clue that I was actually a sixteen-year-old sitting in my bedroom in my parents' house in Lower Hutt.

'In my last year of high school I got a slot on TV One's *Breakfast* show on Tuesday mornings as the youth affairs reporter — so I would get up at 5.30 a.m., take the train into Wellington, and be on air at 7.20 a.m. Then, I'd get changed into my school uniform in the corridor outside the studio, walk back to the railway station, take the train out to Upper Hutt and walk in the school gates just as the bell rang. People in my class would be talking about what I'd said on TV that morning. How weird is that?'

As Jehan told me this, I couldn't get over what a flex it must've been. Seriously, imagine you're battling away in year 11 English, and meanwhile the guy next to you is writing for the country's biggest papers — and there's no forgetting about him, because every Tuesday morning his mug is staring back at you from the TV screen as you drag your sorry self out of bed and eat your Weet-Bix. For Jehan, though, there was plenty more going on inside, as there is for most people in high school.

'Looking back, I really hated myself as a teenager. I wasn't good at sports, and I was super-skinny. I was very socially insecure. I grew up in a Sri Lankan family, and that was tough, because New Zealand was much less diverse — and much less accepting — back in the 1990s. At school, I always felt different to everyone else, and I found it hard to find my place.

'But at a young age, I learnt that I could make up for those things by achieving. I realised I could ask the best questions in class, I could communicate, and I could sometimes make people laugh. When I started to build a media career in my teens, that gave me something to build my identity around. It became my main source of validation. I thought, "If I can perform really well, then I can impress people. That will allow me to bury my self-hatred, and prove to other people that I'm good enough."

This makes sense to me — I've met quite a few people who are immensely successful, but who are also insecure and cling to their achievements to reassure themselves of their value and worth as a person. At its core, it is a type of avoidant coping strategy — a Band-Aid over the top to avoid the need to address the challenges within. As such it doesn't really work — the only option is to try to deal with the issues that lie underneath.

But in his late teens and early twenties, Jehan wasn't ready to confront his feelings of shame and self-doubt. Instead, he kept building his career, which went from strength to strength.

'I worked on *Breakfast* for three years, *Close Up* for three years, and *Seven Sharp* for three years. I had a great life in Wellington, I was travelling around the country, I had a great flat and community, life was awesome. But I was wondering what was next for me. I was given the opportunity to move to Auckland to work on the *Sunday* current affairs programme. It was the most respected show at TVNZ. The reporters were titans of journalism, they had covered wars, they had been all over the world — and I was given the chance to work alongside them at the age of twenty-six, which was huge.

'I got to Auckland and began to find my feet in a new city, which wasn't easy — I didn't know many people, and I found my work environment quite challenging. After six months, I realised I was depressed. I spent the next three years trying every tool in the mental-health toolbox — counselling, antidepressants, reducing stress, cutting back on alcohol, changing my diet, yoga, TED talks, mindfulness, everything in between. But rather than improving, I found myself going deeper and deeper into this hole — until I was suicidal. But from the outside, I still had a very high-functioning life, winning journalism awards, reporting from overseas, interviewing senior politicians. I felt like a fraud, partly because I was hosting TVNZ's first mental-health series and interviewing people about their struggles, but no one had any idea that the host of the show was suicidal.

'After four years of depression, I knew that what I was doing wasn't working. Something had to change. I needed a circuit-breaker. I went to TVNZ and asked for six months of unpaid leave. I moved back to Wellington, because I wanted to be closer to friends and family. I didn't know how I was going to put myself back together, but I knew I needed some time and space to focus on myself. During that time, I wrote a book called *This Is Not How It Ends*, about my mental-health journey. I decided to leave TVNZ and reinvent myself as a public speaker and a mental-health advocate. That's what I've been doing for the last five years.'

Whilst managing mental health is always an ongoing effort, it's fair to say that Jehan is in a much better place now than he has been before. I wanted to understand what had enabled him to get through not only the adversity of this period of mental distress, as he calls it, but also all of the challenges and adversity he has come up against in the immensely successful career he forged at such a young age. I know it can't have been easy.

'I grew up in a Christian family and my faith has always been a really important part of my life. Having a faith doesn't mean you can avoid struggles. In fact, my faith has taught me that suffering is a guaranteed part of life. None of us can escape pain — even though Instagram influencers make us think we can. Experiencing pain doesn't mean that I'm broken or defective. It means I'm human. I'm still loved, and I understand that my pain is not permanent. It doesn't define me.

'In Western cultures, we're not very good at talking about spirituality. But I think it's really important to ask yourself, "What does spirituality look like for me?" That includes your identity, your values, your belief system — the things that help you to make sense of the chaotic world we live in. What does it look like to be spiritually healthy? How could your spiritual health influence your mental health?'

For Jehan, a big part of his ability to be resilient has also come from resolving things that were impacting his wellbeing — and continuing to work on those things to this day.

'A lot of young people who come from ethnic backgrounds carry an invisible sense of shame. It took me years to realise that my relationship with my culture was preventing me from respecting myself. Growing up, I experienced racism and bias which made me try to suppress my culture. But as an adult, I've learnt how to be proud of who I am, and proud of my identity as a New Zealand-born Sri Lankan.

'But that's not always easy. I speak to businesses around the country, and it's not uncommon for me to stand on the stage for an hour in front of a room where not a single other face looks like mine — and that can be really isolating. You might think it shouldn't be. After all, I'm being paid to be there, and I have the stage to myself. But sometimes, I still feel inadequate and out of place. Just like when I was five years old, and a girl in my class said to me, "Are you brown because you don't shower?"'

Finally, reflecting on his whole story and what has been key in getting to this point in his life, Jehan gave me some of the best advice I heard throughout the course of writing this book: 'There's a field of research called narrative psychology, which says that each of us is both the main character in our own story, and the author of it — my story is about me, but I'm also in charge of writing it. I know from my own mental-health journey, and the experiences of hundreds of people I've interviewed, that people who overcome really tough stuff do so by changing the story inside their head. The story that tells them: Who am I? Where have I come from? Where am I going in life?

'My dream is that every young person in New Zealand grows up with the understanding that they are the author of their own story. Even if you can't change your circumstances, even if you can't erase the bad stuff that's happened, you're always the author of your own story. That story is not fixed — it's always in draft form. This is a life-changing idea that most people have never been exposed to. Rewriting your story can have a profound impact on your relationships, your productivity, how you feel about yourself, and how you experience the world.

'The most powerful question I've asked as a journalist — and I've asked thousands — is this: "How can I tell a different story with the same facts?" Because even when you can't change the facts, you can always change the story — and I'm living proof that this can make all the difference.'

# 8

# FIND YOUR MEANING IN LIFE

In my opinion, the best years of school were the ones where you could find the answer to any question you're asked using the internet — before teachers start wanting you to 'show your working'. Before the dawn of AI, this 'show your working' phase marked a pretty abrupt transition where you went from being able to do your homework in about ten minutes of solid copy/pasting of answers, to actually having to do the work, which took me considerably longer — probably because I'd spent the years prior using Google instead of my brain. Lucky you if you're at school now — AI can not only give you the answer, but it can give you the working to make it look like you came up with the answer, too! But as good as the internet is, there are a few questions it can't answer, and one of those is 'What is the meaning of life?'

I can imagine what you're thinking — wow, that got heavy all of a sudden. What the hell does the meaning of life have to do with me, or resilience, or anything for that matter? Who cares? But far from the search for the meaning of life being some big, fancy, grandiose concept that has nothing to do with you, it's actually pretty relevant and close to home.

As humans, we automatically seek and attribute meaning to all aspects of life, including the most trivial: belief in superstitions, charms and luck are all examples of us trying to find meaning in the things that happen to us. We just don't like the fact that life is pretty much mind-bogglingly random and incomprehensible, so our brains constantly try, in whatever way they can, to find patterns and meaning in the chaos. But the problem is that when it comes to the overall meaning of life, it's not just the internet that doesn't have the answer — no one does really.

Here's a better question then: what if, instead, we turn our search inwards and look to find our own individual purpose or meaning — asking not so much 'Why are *we* here?', but rather 'Why am *I* here?', or perhaps even, 'Since I am here, what should I do with myself?' Not 'What is the meaning of life?', but 'What is the meaning of *my* life?'

The funny thing about a question like that is that you're either pretty sure you've got the answer, or you've got absolutely no clue — there's not really any in between. Like most young people, you're probably on the side of having no clue, and that's perfectly fine. I'm not here to tell you that you *have* to find some meaning for your life *now*, or that you're behind schedule. But it's certainly worth some thought, because some form of meaning in your life isn't going to appear out of nowhere. You're going to have to put some thought into the meaning of life, or the meaning of *your* life, or *your* meaning in life, or how to live a life of meaning — which are all slightly different things — because otherwise you're not likely to find it. You'll just stroll right past the signs and clues along the way and potentially miss the turn you should have taken. You don't have to actively seek out meaning, you've just got to be open to finding it. And there's no better time to start than now.

I reckon I've found my meaning in life: I just want to help people. I want to hopefully assist them to improve in some way, and for them to then go on and improve the world themselves. Of course, as you've probably guessed, this wasn't always what I thought my meaning was — rather, it's something I've only discovered by stumbling into the opportunities that cancer has provided me.

Before the cancer, I thought my meaning in life was 'success' — which I guess in some ways is still my meaning in life now, but then I meant the traditional Western definition of success, like you see in the movies. I wanted a job as a lawyer or a banker — any high-status job, really, where I could wear a suit and drive an expensive car. I wanted to gather a body of evidence which would prove to others around me that I was successful.

I'm not saying there is anything wrong with that — in fact, I think that's probably one of the most common goals of young people. I'm just saying that while I believed that's what I wanted at the time, since then I've come to realise that material success wasn't actually what drives me the most. Sure, if material success transpires along the way then that's great, but first I'd much rather focus on taking the opportunity that I've been given to help others in some small way, whether that's public speaking or charity work or this book, because I find that far more rewarding. I'm no more qualified nor altruistic than anyone else, I'm just especially driven and motivated by these goals in particular — as a result of the values which we discussed in the last chapter. Material success has shifted from being the starting point in my thinking, to being the end point or product of what I want to do most. It feels good to have stumbled across this realisation, even if it came about through having to go through cancer.

.........

So, what's the point of meaning anyway? Why do you need to know your purpose in life, other than being super-organised? And what does it have to do with resilience? Well, it comes back to psychology.

Considering your life has a meaning or greater purpose has been proven to have a significant positive impact on your overall wellbeing. Research shows that those people who have a sense of meaning flourish and succeed and, without meaning in their lives, people suffer. As well as that, it's proven to have a really powerful impact on your resilience when adversity strikes.

Believing your life has a meaning creates a whole heap of positive emotion because, well, it's a positive thing. If you feel like you've got something to live for, or the ability to create an impact, how do you feel? Good, right? American psychologist Michael Steger, the founder and director of the Center for Meaning and Purpose at Colorado State University, puts it this way:

> 'Valuing one's life, having a sense of direction and purpose, and being able to comprehend one's experience seem contradictory to many manifestations of psychological distress.'

English translation: You don't feel bad things as strongly or as often if you feel your life has a purpose or meaning.

That's the 'with it, people flourish and succeed' element. The flip side is the 'without it, people suffer'. How do you feel if you think your life doesn't have any greater purpose or meaning, that you are an unwitting passenger on a ride you didn't sign up for, that you have no control over the world at large and no ability to make an impact? Not good, right?

This part is fairly simple, and without diminishing the work of countless people far brighter than me into a single line: *of course good things in your life will make you feel good, and not having good things will make you feel bad*. Meaning isn't just a good thing, it's an essential part of human existence.

The second part is my favourite though: the profound and positive impact having a sense of meaning has on your resilience. In short, *having meaning gives you an extra layer of armour against adversity*. It's the extra bit of fuel you need in the tank to get to the petrol station when you're already below E. It's the spare change you find in the bottom of your bag on the day you forget your lunch.

There's a very well-known book called *Man's Search for Meaning*, written by a psychiatrist and neurologist called Viktor Frankl. Frankl was a Holocaust survivor, and much of his life's work was based around what he learnt about the psychology of survival in concentration camps. In these camps, many of the male prisoners were worked to death: that is, rather than simply being killed in a systematic way, they were first forced to work themselves to the brink, doing impossible hours of physical labour in inhumane environments with just enough food and water to avoid immediate death, then once they were burnt out and unable to go on, they were killed. However, some of these workers, including Frankl himself, survived. Among the prisoners who died, some survived only a short time and others a longer period of time. Frankl sought to find out what it was that enabled some people to survive longer than others around them, to keep moving forwards in the face of indescribable hardship — was it their age, previous career, fitness level? No. The thing he identified which was the greatest indicator of someone's odds of survival in a death camp was a sense of meaning in life.

The reason that meaning provides this buffer, this extra boost of resilience, is a phenomenon called *transcendence*. Basically, transcendence is the idea that even in a challenging period or a moment of adversity, *you're able to get through it because you can see the bigger picture*. You can look *beyond* the immediate difficulty because your life has a greater purpose than the challenge you're existing within right now.

In a tricky situation, you can think, 'Wow, this sucks — but I'll hang in there because . . .':

- I've been through things this tough, or nearly this tough, or tougher, before.

- I'm going through this for a purpose, an outcome which I want to achieve.
- This is just a moment of suffering in a broader picture of life (an activity which, undeniably, has more than a few moments of suffering).

Transcendence is a seriously powerful thing. It basically allows you to tune out much of the challenge and suffering which you're facing in the present moment for the purpose of the greater good — because you know that what you're going through right now will lead to something positive in the future.

So, for example:

- I can get through this fitness test because it will allow me to make the team.
- I can study and get through this exam because it will pave my way into my dream job.
- I can get through this shitty day at work because it will allow me to support my family, who are the most important thing to me.

If you take meaning away from those scenarios, what are you left with? A shitty fitness test, a shitty exam, and a shitty day at work. It's not hard to see how meaning is critical to your ability to overcome adversity.

This is the part where I could whip out my cancer as the perfect example — to tell you how I look back on my time going through cancer and remember the exact moment, as I lay in a hospital bed with tears streaming down my face, that I said, 'Hey, I'm going to get through this because, after all this horrible treatment is over, I will be able to do something that feels really meaningful with my life. This adversity will give me a whole bunch of lessons and stories which I can, in turn, pass on to other people to positively impact them and help them. I can do this, I just know I can' — as motivational music swelled in the background.

This motivational moment never happened. The reality is that, at the time, that's not at all what I thought, and it's not what enabled me to get through my cancer experience. Actually, it was the *suffering* which made me want to get through the cancer.

I wonder if you raised your eyebrows before when I mentioned Frankl, and his discovery that a sense of meaning was the single greatest predictor of someone's survival in a concentration camp. How could anyone find meaning in a concentration camp, or meaning in life, when facing near-certain death? When family and loved ones are gone, and there's no hope on the horizon? Where the hell were they finding this meaning?

That was another of Frankl's theories — the idea of suffering *in itself* as a form of meaning: that pain, adversity and going through hell give us a reason to fight on. He wrote about the fact that a person's *attitude towards suffering* can become a form of meaning in itself. In other words, making an effort to be brave and strong, to summon up courage and hold on to a positive attitude in the face of immense challenges, can provide you with a sense of meaning and a way of overcoming those exact challenges. To quote him directly:

> 'The way in which a man accepts his fate and all the suffering it entails, the way in which he takes up his cross, gives him ample opportunity — even under the most difficult circumstances — to add a deeper meaning to his life. It may remain brave, dignified and unselfish. Or in the bitter fight for self-preservation he may forget his human dignity and become no more than an animal. Here lies the chance for a man to either make use of or to forgo the opportunities of attaining the moral values that a difficult situation may afford him.'

In other words, the meaning of suffering is to keep your head held high and to not crumble in the face of challenge, nor lose your self-respect — a worthy challenge undoubtedly, and a form of meaning and purpose.

That doesn't mean that it's wrong to feel broken by your circumstances, or to suffer and experience normal human emotion through adversity. But it does tell us that the suffering itself can provide us with a sense of meaning and purpose which can in turn help us to fight on, even and *especially* when there might not seem like there's anything else to cling on to.

Back on the hospital ward, this experience of what was largely dreadful suffering became my first-ever chance to utilise suffering as a form of meaning. Getting through the treatment and back to 'not treatment', getting through this cycle of chemo, getting through this day of chemo, getting through this *bag* of chemo, getting through this wave of nausea, became the sole focus of my existence. Not because it would allow me to go on and help others, not because it would allow me to survive — but just because it was my reality, and I had no other options.

If I was going to go through adversity, I wanted to do so as graciously as possible and with my head held high. A bit like what I said earlier about laughing in the face of adversity to reduce its power, it brought me satisfaction to outlast a sensation of great discomfort, be that physical or mental, to be flexible and adaptable enough to cope. To quote Frankl one final time, it is 'the uniquely human potential at its best, which is to transform a personal tragedy into a triumph, to turn one's predicament into a human achievement. When we are no longer able to change a situation . . . we are challenged to change ourselves.' That was a huge part of how I got through my cancer — *because I saw the suffering as a form of meaning, an opportunity, instead of something I was just being subjected to and forced to endure against my will.*

This attitude is not confined to people in concentration camps or hospitals — it is an approach to one of the only constants in life: adversity, in almost any context. It tells us that in our deepest and darkest and most challenging moments, we will be provided with a greater supply of motivation and purpose than ever before. And if you can find a way to turn the *adversity* that you're facing in life into the *meaning* that you have in life, then you've got a self-constructing bridge over troubled waters.

This first experience of using suffering and adversity as a form of meaning and purpose, while I was in hospital, has gone on to be more influential and impactful in my life than I ever expected — and not just when it comes to facing up to things which have gone wrong. My passion for endurance sport came about solely as a result of having gone through my cancer treatment. In getting through my treatment, I learnt that not only was my body capable of enduring more than I could have ever imagined, and that my mind was the key to being able to do so, but that the emotions you experience when you overcome or outlast something challenging are really, powerfully positive — in fact, the greater the challenge, the greater the emotion. That allows you to find meaning in suffering. To be clear, I don't spend hours running or cycling because I'm having fun — I do it because when I stop, I feel satisfied with what I've achieved. I've made meaning from the suffering.

Frankl's assurance that greater adversity can provide greater meaning keeps me running in the forest for another hour (even though I'm plainly not having fun at the time) because I know this adversity (and getting through it) will make me happy later.

•••••••••

Okay, you say, so meaning impacts my ability to be happy and be resilient. But what if I haven't found my meaning yet? Where do I even start?

I know that, as a young person, being asked to try to figure out, for instance, what job you want to do is challenging enough without me asking you about your purpose or meaning in life — not to mention that you haven't yet had much of an opportunity to get out and explore the world. Here's the good news, though:

> You don't need to figure out what your whole purpose in life is, you just have to figure out what your purpose in life is right now.

Research tells us that people's perceived meaning or purpose in life changes significantly over their lifetime. As we grow and develop, our perceived meaning changes based on what we want the most: as young people, we tend to most value fun and enjoyment, middle-aged people tend to seek out achievement and establishment, and in later life we tend to desire social integration and connection. It's not necessarily possible to explain what your whole purpose in life is, because, for most people, what gives them that purpose will change significantly throughout their life.

So, rather than facing the humongous bastard of a question 'What is your purpose in life?', let's ask:

- What do you want to be doing with your life right now?
- What matters to you right now?
- What do you value right now?

Hopefully, something comes to mind for you. Maybe it doesn't. And that's okay — just let those thoughts percolate away in your brain.

Interestingly, your meaning does not have to be, and in fact may well *not* be, something you are good at or something you spend most of your time on. When I was a teenager, before my cancer diagnosis, I was undoubtedly preoccupied with having a good time. If I had looked a little bit deeper, though, at my constant desire to socialise, I would've seen that my goal was actually connection with people, which ties into what I perceive my current purpose in life to be. I wanted to be with people, and I wanted to be having fun with them.

For others, their purpose and focus in life right now might be sport, art, or a cultural activity like music or another type of performance. It might be connection with friends and people like it was for me. Spending time in the outdoors, or gaming, or chess. *Whatever is important to you is important.* It's more important for you to have *something* in your life which you care about and which you place effort into, than what that thing actually is.

Research also tells us that people who have intrinsically (internally) motivated goals rather than extrinsically (externally) motivated goals tend to be happier in life. That is to say, people whose meaning revolves around connectedness, impact or a sense of purpose are happier than those whose meaning leads to extrinsic goals, like wealth accumulation, status or prestige. The good news is that most goals can be viewed from either angle. For instance, wanting to achieve sporting success because it will make you proud of yourself, rather than because it'll impress other people, will make you happier in the long run. It's all about what you look for within your own goals and achievements.

Writer and mental-health advocate Jehan Casinader has some wise words for people looking to find meaning in their work and life:

> 'My advice to young people is to find something that you're passionate about, and set yourself an almost impossible goal that

> forces you to chase after it. You won't find yourself with a lot of time on your hands, but it will give you something to anchor your life.
>
> 'In some ways, I regret how hard I worked in my teens. I would have liked to be more chilled out, to have had more fun, and not be so obsessed with achievement, because those are precious years and you can't get them back. But I don't really regret the choices I made, because they gave me fifteen years of incredible experiences as a journalist. That would never have happened if I just sat around waiting for someone to ring me up and give me my big break.
>
> 'But you also have to be careful that your work doesn't become your whole identity. You have to be confident in who you are, regardless of your achievements.'

For some of you, there will be nothing which comes to mind as a greater purpose or meaning to your life at this point. And that's absolutely fine. The reality is that meaning is not something which just appears before you, but is something which everyone has to create for themselves at some point, when they have the right set of circumstances and opportunities. That time will come for you.

One really good place to start is taking another look at your values (see chapter 7): those things which you're willing to get into an argument over are probably things which matter to you, and consequently they are probably things which would stand up as pieces of meaning or purpose in your life. Here are some more starting points from which you can work out what your purpose might be:

- What matters to you?
- What are your strengths?
- What gives you energy and excitement, and what takes it away?
- What do you enjoy in life, and why do you enjoy it?

Often, you can find your purpose or meaning just by digging down a little deeper into what you enjoy and asking *why* you enjoy it. I enjoy public speaking, but public speaking isn't my *purpose* — I have to go one layer deeper to find I enjoy it because my purpose is connection and helping others. Do you enjoy sport because you like teamwork? Do you enjoy history because you want to understand why the world is the way it is today? Do you enjoy art because you value creative expression and looking at things differently, or drama because you want to move and impact people through your performance?

## Summary

That's that, then. Go off and find out the meaning of your life. Before you leave, let's just remind ourselves that it's not some fluffy, airy-fairy thing we're talking about: it's a real and powerful force.

Let's also keep in mind that you don't need to know the answer yet. It is simply about having an open mind and being open to discovering your purpose — an awareness that there is something out there for you, and rather than it dropping into your lap, you'll have to put in a bit of effort to find it yourself.

You need to have something to strive towards, to build your goals and focus in life around. The reason is simple: if you have an outcome to work towards, you can find almost any way to get there.

Perceiving meaning in your life connects you with other people, creates positive emotions and gives you drive, but not only that — it enables you to fare better during times of adversity, too. When things are tough, you're able to see the bigger picture — to see that the tough times are just part of a journey towards your larger goal or purpose — and so you are better able to outlast them. Not only can this sense of meaning allow you to get through the tough times, it can actually make them quite rewarding.

That's great for helping you face everyday struggles — study, or assignments, or sports. But what about big adversity? What is the possible meaning that can allow you to overcome the death of a loved one, or cancer, or being in a concentration camp? How can there be any sense of meaning in that level of suffering?

Remember that, in times of adversity, even when you don't think you can find any meaning or purpose, suffering and adversity can be a form of meaning in itself — a challenge to face and overcome while remaining as much of an upstanding person as you were before the adversity. The 'meaning' is to not be broken by your circumstances, and instead to stand fast in the storm of suffering. The greater the suffering, the greater the challenge, and the greater the satisfaction in overcoming it. In our greatest and deepest challenges, there is a hidden store of meaning and purpose which can still be tapped, if you view suffering through this lens.

## Zoe Hobbs — The Power of Purpose

Zoe Hobbs is the fastest-ever Kiwi woman over 100 metres. She's also the fastest-ever woman in Oceania, and the only woman in Oceania to ever run 100 metres in under 11 seconds. She is one of the finest running talents New Zealand has ever produced. But if we just define her achievements by how fast she runs, we're missing a whole lot more.

The sport of sprinting requires a mountain of confidence and self-belief. If you've ever watched the 100-metres final at the Olympics, you'll know there's far more time spent flexing and playing up for the cameras than there is running, because generally only sprinters with that level of self-belief make it to the top. As Zoe told me: 'Especially in this sport, your mental capacity has just as much impact as your physical capacity.'

Maybe because of that, much of our chat was about self-belief and the role it plays in Zoe's ability to be resilient and perform at such a high level. I knew that, to get so far in the sport, she'd have to back herself. So it was a surprise when one of the first things Zoe said was, 'Throughout my time in this sport, I've probably always had more self-doubt than self-belief.

'Growing up, I always had this desire to one day compete in the Commonwealth Games and Olympic Games as a sprinter. And for me to even voice that when I was younger took courage, because I always felt there would be doubt from my peers around me.

'Sprinting in New Zealand is a non-traditional event — typically it's more common for our distance runners or throwers to be successful, or even on the world stage at all — so there was some resistance and pushback in my journey to becoming a sprinter and competing at a world-class level. People attempted to convince me that the best chance I'd have of making it onto the world stage would be to pursue virtually anything other than the individual 100 metres. I had graphs put in front of me during my development years showing my progression and how it had plateaued over the 100-metre distance, followed up with attempts to convince me to put my focus into the 200 metres or to start taking up hurdles. You know when you can sense doubt when people ask you what you're doing or why you're doing it. I felt that in my pursuit all the time in the early days — how can you not? You can imagine what that does to the confidence and self-belief of an aspiring athlete who's choosing that pathway.'

Clearly, though, other people's doubts didn't stop Zoe. With the independence which came from being a boarder at high school, she often had to lean on her own initiative, drive and work ethic to get her training done. 'Throughout my teenage years, I often felt torn between two realities. Growing up, I hadn't witnessed anyone from New Zealand compete in the event I wanted to pursue on the world stage, so it felt like a bold move to put as much energy and focus into it as I did. I feared I would look back in life and regret the sacrifices I'd made for my sport, especially if I never "made it". I remember thinking that I would have to make up for all the lost social years, the times that I missed out on as a young person growing up, after my retirement from sport — when I would be finally able to live a "normal" life.

'I always had this view, driven by society, that your teenage years are the years that are meant to be the most fun — and that fun seems to largely be defined as partying and drinking. When I went to uni, I wasn't your typical student who was out drinking every weekend. For me, that was rare, or at least a calculated decision, usually only during off-season breaks or special occasions.

'I now look back and thank my younger self for having committed throughout those years because it all built up to where I am now. I've got zero regrets over making those sacrifices — it gave me so much more drive and a reason to be successful in my pursuit.'

Zoe has Māori ancestry, through her maternal grandmother, and I was keen to ask about how her whakapapa, her Māori heritage, might have contributed to her resilience. When I did so, I felt like I'd accidentally uncovered yet another area where Zoe had been made to doubt herself and who she is.

'At our primary school, I was one of few brown kids, and that did have an impact on how I viewed myself. I did feel a bit out of place at times, and I felt a bit of racism at times growing up, which was very different to my brother's experience; he was more fair-skinned with blond hair when he was younger.

'For me, that manifested in not being proud of who I was. I think that experience of racism fed into not wanting to associate with the culture and the language when I was younger.'

When Zoe said this, I felt a strong sense of empathy — not, to be clear, because I've ever experienced any discrimination, but because as a teenager, all I wanted was to fit in — and yet, despite being a pretty average guy, completely unremarkable in almost every way, I'd felt so incredibly insecure and self-conscious anyway. I couldn't imagine how Zoe had managed to deal with being made to feel 'othered' at a time of life when she was already so highly attuned to what other people thought.

'I think one of the hard things about it was not wanting to be seen as that serious person who takes everything personally, which is often what I felt in these situations where I'd feel offended. People would make jokes or say certain things, but I wouldn't want to be called the serious person, so I'd just roll with it and laugh along with them.'

Zoe cries as she talks about the intergenerational impact of colonisation on her whānau. 'My nana, Tahanga Paraha, also known as Elise MacLeod, grew up at a time when speaking te reo at school was prohibited and she was forced to change her name to an English name (Elise Paraha). From a young age, Nana had to adapt her way of living to the Western world, as the only world she knew (te ao Māori) was not celebrated or acknowledged within society. Naturally, this continued throughout her motherhood journey, which resulted in our whānau losing our connection and our knowledge fading. It wasn't until after she sadly passed away my cousin discovered she was given a different name at birth. This caused a lot of confusion as to why this was never spoken about within our whānau. Now that we have put the pieces of the puzzle together, it's clear why she felt it wasn't an important thing to share. It saddens me that we grew up with little exposure to Māori culture and customs as well as not learning te reo before

Nana's passing. For me, I still have so much learning to do, but I am proud to be Māori and am on a journey to reconnect with what was lost.'

If you watch Zoe race on the world stage, you'll pretty quickly notice a contrast. While many athletes preen and dance around when they're introduced in front of the camera, Zoe tends to offer a small smile and a wave. And then she runs really, really fast.

'I think part of it is not wanting to be outwardly confident. I was raised to always be humble, but I'm only now starting to explore the difference between being humble and being shut down by tall poppy syndrome. I think, if you're doing well, you should be able to be proud of your results and talk about them. I have a lot of respect for people who are proud of what they've achieved, and who are confident in what they're going after. You can do that and still be humble at the same time — they're not two different things.

'But I notice that I'm still stuck in that whole tall poppy mentality. If I'm talking in the media, I'm always focused on not making it sound like I'm up myself or too confident. I'm quite considered in how I say things, which I think is ridiculous, because I should be able to be confident in saying what I want to achieve without playing things down. I'm always conscious of that and am working on letting go of this.'

Zoe must have started to turn the tide on her lack of self-belief and wrestle back control over her doubts, or she never could have made it this far. Her self-belief seems to have started with a setback which would have broken a lesser athlete.

'I guess a key moment for me was missing out on the Tokyo Olympics.' In 2021, despite running the World Athletics qualifying time, Zoe was not selected to represent New Zealand at the Olympics due to New Zealand's rule that, in addition to making the qualifying time, athletes should be 'capable of a top 16 finish'.

Imagine seeing the rankings list, knowing that you're inside the quota to get the nod from World Athletics for an invitation to the Olympics, and then being told by your own country that they don't think you're up to the task. This wasn't a case of there being a better Kiwi sprinter than Zoe — New Zealand didn't enter anyone in the women's 100 metres at Tokyo.

Zoe is remarkably level-headed about it in hindsight. 'I took a huge mental hit after not making that team and spiralled even deeper into self-doubt. I began to question why I was even doing the sport. Am I ever going to make it? Am I good enough? No, I'm not good enough. I took the time I needed to work through that, and really reflected on why I was doing this. That brought me back to the fundamental reason why I was doing it in the first place: I love the sport. I decided to shift my mentality away from negativity, to try to take the pressure off myself, and to focus on enjoying the training, enjoying the process of doing it with my training squad, and simply enjoying the sport. And I think that's when I started to see the results. I started to see some progress, and with this sport being so measurable, that became addictive and I got on a good roll.

'I think the biggest thing that helped me overcome that self-doubt was to see small, gradual improvements over and over again, until they built up to where I'm at now. The resilience needed to get here purely came from my love of athletics.

'Despite the challenges, the value that the sport brought into my life in many different ways was enough to keep me in it. I didn't know where I was going to end up, I didn't know if I would end up making it to this level. I just did it because it was something that I loved and it was something I was good at — and to me, it seemed a waste to throw that away. I am very blessed to have this ability to run fast, but I knew it would take commitment and hard work to get me to the places I wanted. I would hate to look back and think, "What if? What could have happened if I had actually committed to that pathway?" And so now, to be here, beyond where I ever thought it would go, is just such a privilege.'

To me, it sounds like it was finding a sense of purpose which gave Zoe the resilience to keep going. Her passion for the pursuit and the sport, along with a tight team and capturing the small wins and successes along the way, kept her going long after others would have stopped. But maybe for Zoe, the challenges, the adversity and the suffering were all part of that purpose as well.

'I think being challenged is a good thing because it's an opportunity to learn, and through learning, you get better. I think the more challenges or adversity you go through, the better person you become. Every challenge offers something to learn and reflect on, and you can use it as something to really grow from and do better next time.

'I think, if I hadn't been through any adversity to get where I am now, my achievements wouldn't feel half as good. The most rewarding thing for me is looking back at the journey and knowing how far I've come and what I had to make it through to get here. That's the thing that fills me with immense joy and satisfaction, more than the actual results: it comes more from knowing where I started and where I am now.

'If I could go back, I would tell my younger self that the little voices in my head that were scared of failure and scared of the way I would be viewed if I didn't succeed were so wrong. Giving something a crack and committing to it regardless of the outcome is so much more admirable than being the person who just gives up.'

9

# SELF-CARE: HELP YOURSELF TO BE RESILIENT

As well as the mental tools we have been talking about, there are a few physical aspects of your lifestyle that can help to make you more resilient, by getting you in better mental shape for tackling adversity. I really don't want this to feel like compulsory reading for health class, and please know I'm not going to lecture you, because I couldn't even if I tried. As you'll soon read, I don't think I did a good job of a single one of these areas when I was a teenager, so I'm hardly in a position to tell you what you should or shouldn't do. That's not what this is — rather, it's just me giving you some information in case it's helpful for you, because in all honesty it would be careless of me to write a book about resilience without including some things which we know play a really big role in your ability to be resilient.

## Exercise

You know that kid who gets picked last for teams in PE? And when they do get picked, the whole team groans? Hey, that was me!

For most of my time at school, I absolutely hated exercise, and because of that I also hated sport, and all the hype around it. I forged sick notes, feigned shin splits, growing pains and ingrown toenails, and really was about as un-resilient as you can possibly get in my attempts to avoid sport and exercise — because I sucked at it, and I didn't like that. It was hard, and it hurt, and I was bad at it — so why would I choose to put myself in that position? I still remember finishing my last ever PE lesson in year 10, knowing I wasn't taking it in year 11, and feeling so satisfied that no one would ever make me run again for the rest of my life.

Since then, well . . . things have changed, and exercise is now one of the most important parts of my life, in large part because of how good it is for my overall resilience and wellbeing. But it wasn't until quite recently that I discovered the science behind why that is — and how much evidence there is for its benefits.

.........

Exercise hurts, particularly if it's quite intense, right? Lungs burning, muscles on fire — and, in my case, both your opponents and teammates laughing at you. To cut a long story short (one you need a medical degree to understand), our brain doesn't like this physical feeling, so it finds a way to cope. It can't *stop* the pain, so instead it pumps out a type of neurotransmitter called endorphins, which interact with the receptors in your brain which perceive pain. They clog them up and prevent the signal of pain from being received by the brain — like taking a natural painkiller.

Pretty cool, right? But not necessarily all that useful for us, because when you've got a headache it's far easier to take a Panadol than go for a run. But the really interesting part, and the reason I'm writing about this, is because the receptors in the brain which register physical pain are the same ones which register mental pain — and therefore, endorphins have the same impact on your mental discomfort as they do on your physical pain.

This is exactly what happens when you exercise: your ability to feel negative emotions is reduced, and so their effect is dulled. You don't have to just take my word for it: it's science, fact, physiology — not a sometimes, not a maybe. It is *every* time, for *every* person. And because of this effect, studies have shown that regular exercise can be at least as effective, and sometime more effective, as medication for treating mild to moderate depression — which seems completely crazy when you stop and think about it.

But what if you don't have mild depression, or moderate depression, or any depression at all? What if, in fact, you feel pretty good? What's the point in exercising then? Well, medical journal *The Lancet* published a study in 2018 which showed that these benefits are universal, no matter how happy you were to start with, or how good your life was anyway.

Using a sample size of 1.2 million people — which is absolutely *gigantic* for a study of this type — they matched people of the same age, gender, race, religion, socio-economic status and so on, basically pairing people up with their exact twin: except that one of them exercised for 45 minutes, three times a week and the other one didn't.

> The study found that people who exercised reported on average 43.2 per cent fewer days where they felt bad, or felt their mental health was negative, than people who didn't.

Let that sink in: *you can make your life feel nearly twice as good by exercising a few days a week*. To put that in perspective, multiple studies have shown that people who win the lottery don't report their life improving anywhere near that much. You seriously have to consider what other change in your life could make you have 43 per cent fewer bad days, because apart from exercising regularly, there's probably not a lot else — not even winning Lotto. Even if things aren't bad, *exercise will still make things better*.

The other benefit, from the perspective of resilience, is that so much of sport and physical exercise is about facing challenges and adversity — competition, risk, failure, disappointments, negative emotions — and finding meaning and satisfaction in the suffering, like I talked about earlier. Between the stress, setbacks, challenges and prolonged discomfort, sport is, really, just a form of manufactured adversity — hence why I used to try to hide from it!

But far from this being a reason to shy away from it, it's actually an opportunity to practise and develop your resilience skills. It is a training ground for enhancing skills that will make the rest of your life easier. For that reason alone, you should be doing it. And if, like me as a teenager, you don't want to because you hate it, then all the better, *all the more reason to do it*, because it will build more resilience. It's far from a bad thing to have something in your life that you suck at but can live with and even enjoy, because it's one significant way you can learn to be resilient before other challenges start coming your way.

Coming back to what I was saying earlier, though, all this didn't matter to me a few years ago — because nothing, and certainly none of the things mentioned above, would have got me to do sport. So, I hear you. But now, through some friendly encouragement, a few opportunities, and seeing the benefits it had in my life, I'm far better at incorporating exercise into my life in a way the old me would be horrified by.

Now that I exercise regularly, I know that if I *don't* exercise, I don't feel as positive, as clear-headed or as productive. Because of that, it's now a non-negotiable for me. I do go through stages where I'm a bit slack, but generally I'll run or cycle four or five days a week. Coming from the guy who celebrated never having to do PE again, you can only imagine how positive the impact must be for me to willingly choose to do it almost every day.

Speaking of that person I used to be, there are a few things I wish I'd known back then:

1. You don't have to do a lot — a little beats none, a million times over. There were times when I thought about dabbling with exercise but running for less than ten minutes was legitimately all I could manage, and I didn't want to do that because I felt like that was embarrassing

— like running for not even ten minutes was a joke. Now I'm pretty fit, I still sometimes go for a run for ten minutes on a busy day because it's better than zero minutes. Don't feel like you don't want to do tiny bits of exercise because you feel it's not going to make a difference, or because your ego says you should be able to do more. It doesn't have to be massive — start small. Jog to the end of your street and back. Walk to the end of your street and back. Do one exercise at the gym. Something beats nothing, hands down.

2. Routine is key. Set aside three days a week to do something — say, decide that Tuesday, Thursday, Saturday, I'll run around the block. The key is being able to follow a routine, because if you can do that, everything else will fall into place. Three days of small activities beats one day of extreme training.
3. Do what you love. I hated the idea of exercise because for me it meant doing something I hated, like running or swimming. But it could be throwing a Frisbee at the park for a bit or kicking a ball around with mates. Find something you actually enjoy. There are lots of different ways to get these benefits, without it having to suck.

## Sleep and Rest

I spent my teenage years staying up as late as I possibly could, just to try to catch up on those traumatic years when I was a kid of being sent to bed while the adults stayed up. Since the day I was first allowed to decide when I went to bed, how much sleep I was meant to get was not even of vague interest to me — and certainly not the science behind it. It's another example of something which we all sort of know and have heard about from teachers, parents, health lessons . . . but again, I either didn't know or didn't care about the scientific evidence behind it until I started my work on resilience.

The short version? A study done by three major universities found that young people who sleep just thirty minutes less each night than their peers are significantly more likely to report poor mental-health outcomes — they're more likely to have depression or anxiety, or to report low mood. As one of the scientists leading the project said:

> 'What we are now seeing is that the relationship between sleep and mental health for teenagers is a two-way street. While poorer sleep habits are associated with worse mental health, we are also seeing how addressing sleep for young people with depression and anxiety can have a big impact on their wellbeing.'*

Looking at it from another angle, studies have shown that people who experience insomnia, or difficulty sleeping, are ten times more likely to have clinical depression and seventeen times more likely to have clinical anxiety than the general population.

* Quoted in University of Reading, 'Poor sleep significantly linked with teenage depression', ScienceDaily (website), 17 June 2020, <sciencedaily.com/releases/2020/06/200617194508.htm>.

So why does this happen? Why is sleep so important? In the case of serious insomnia, it's probably due to the lack of sleep creating chemical imbalances in the brain. Your brain needs sleep to balance out your hormones and all the other chemistry.

In the case of reduced sleep — keeping in mind that thirty minutes less sleep each night is not very much at all — there's probably some kind of cumulative effect. Researchers think it could be related to the reduced sleep increasing hormonal imbalances in the brain, or maybe something as simple as just having less energy to take part in the activities which you enjoy, resulting in a reduced quality of life, which creates less positive emotion and therefore more significant negative mental-health outcomes. Just having that little bit less sleep each night can negatively affect your overall outlook on life, your energy levels and your emotions. There's no solid answer because scientists actually know very little about sleep relative to how much we know about the rest of the human body.

I won't tell you to go and get more sleep, because you're not going to listen to me anyway, just like I wouldn't have listened to someone telling me. I'd just say, I know my quality of life is definitely better when I get an adequate amount of sleep. That's not always possible for me, nor will it be for you — sometimes you'll have assignments or study that need to be done, or social or school engagements that cause late nights.

But if you can begin to take this seriously and build a commitment to sleep into your life, the overall impact will be beneficial to every aspect, from your studies to your social relationships and, as the research shows, your mental health as well.

Here are some things which might help:

1. The people who had significantly better mental-health outcomes in the studies were getting over eight hours' sleep a night. The people who were way more likely to have depression or anxiety were getting seven and a half hours of sleep per night. There isn't a magic number for everyone, but it seems to be that for most young people, at least eight hours is adequate. So, if you're trying to work out a number to strive towards, I think eight is a good place to start.
2. If it's actually the sleeping part that you struggle with, not just not wanting to go to bed, have a look at your 'sleep hygiene'. This basically means the series of habits that you have around going to sleep, including the environment, which are conducive to having good sleep. Some examples are going to sleep and waking up at the same time each day (establishing a routine), not drinking caffeine (coffee, energy drinks, etc.) after twelve o'clock, not lying in bed if you're not trying to sleep, not using your phone before you try to go to sleep, blocking out all light so your room is as dark as possible, keeping the room cool, etc. There are about a hundred different elements to sleep hygiene which you can research, but most of them are pretty simple and you can most likely think of some things you can improve on right now.

I also want to mention something that I really think sends the wrong message. For some reason, some people seem to take a lot of pride in how hard they can work themselves. I've seen this with mates who are at uni and brag about staying up for three days straight doing assignments, or people who start businesses and flex about pulling fifteen-hour work days, seven days a week.

A lot of people seem to really rate this idea of just smashing themselves, but I don't. They think the best way to succeed is doing as many things as possible, as intensely as possible. But aside from destroying your body and just feeling like death warmed up because you're not sleeping enough, this whole philosophy of always being go go go is a fallacy, because it doesn't even make you more productive. Here's a bit of science to prove it.

Have you ever been reading a book, then suddenly realise that you can't remember anything you've been reading for the past few pages? Like the words have been going past but you haven't been processing them? Maybe this is even the third time you've read this exact page.

What's making this happen is your brain is switching between its two operating modes. There's a state called the Task Positive Network (TPN), which is when your brain is processing information, like reading a book, doing an exam, or even scrolling stuff on your phone — basically when your brain is quite active. And then there is something called the Default Mode Network (DMN) which, putting it simply, is daydreaming. When your brain wanders off and you're alone with your thoughts, you're not focused on the outside world, you're on autopilot. It's when someone starts talking to you and you have to ask them to repeat themselves because, 'Sorry, I was zoned out.'

Your brain requires DMN, the downtime, for a certain amount of time each day to maintain peak productivity — which is why your thoughts start to wander sometimes. Your brain is taking the initiative to switch to the DMN process. If you don't take that DMN time, your brain will take it for you, whenever it chooses to, which can be a real pain when you're trying to study and your brain keeps wandering, for instance. That's a decrease in productivity.

If, despite these signs, you *still* don't take the time to zone out, if you force yourself to keep concentrating, then you start to get that brain-fried feeling, where you can't focus or concentrate at all, or you get stuck on a problem. Words don't make sense anymore. This is what happens after big exams, and why your heads feels so fuzzy afterwards — because you can't let your mind wander during exams, although we all know at times it tries to and you end up staring out of the window going into DMN mode.

Why is this all relevant? Well, those people you hear about who wake up at 4 a.m., smash fifteen egg whites and a green smoothie for breakfast, drive to work with an audiobook on in the car, work five hours solid, scroll on their phone over the lunch break (if they bother taking one), work another five hours, smash a gym session with mates, drive home with a podcast on, watch a movie, then go to sleep, *they never get any DMN time*. Their brain is always in that TPN focus mode. Likewise, the mates who study until 3 a.m. and then sleep for four hours and repeat the process, or the entrepreneurs who skite about sleeping under their desk at work. Also, anyone who has ever made even a fleeting mention of 'hustling' or 'the grind' on Insta.

Having your mind racing the whole time can undeniably be satisfying — it feels good to finish an assignment you had to smash out, knowing that you worked hard and did well. But the reality is that science tells us this isn't the most efficient way to work, and it's certainly not the best way in terms of our mental health and resilience. Your brain *needs* bits of this DMN time, and to stop it from taking it whenever it wants, you have to create opportunities for it to do so — moments of the day for you to relax and not be focusing on anything. Otherwise, you'll end up being just a brain-fried mess with no focus or attention span.

You have to find a little time in your day to just let your mind drift and your brain go into DMN. This is really simple to do — some examples are showering, lying in bed before you go to sleep, going for a walk without scrolling on your phone. One thing that *doesn't* count as DMN time is looking at social media, because your brain is still in TPN mode processing information. You're also more likely to achieve DMN when you're doing a task, but something which isn't mentally demanding, like folding washing or doing dishes or walking, as opposed to sitting still and doing nothing. For me, loading or emptying the dishwasher is always a time when I zone out (and no, your mum didn't pay me to say that).

You need to be in your head with your thoughts just flowing by pretty regularly throughout the day — every two hours or so. Think about how your school day is structured: you have a break every ninety minutes or two hours, right? That's not a coincidence.

In practice, this means that you need to be intelligent about how you plan your studying throughout your day, week, year

— doing bits at a time, and not cramming assignments or study, because you're not getting the best out of yourself or doing the best for yourself, scientifically speaking. And you need to be aiming to get those full eight hours of sleep as many nights as you can, by putting some basic actions in place. You're guaranteed to be more efficient and productive, and to have better mental health, if you do.

## Food

Again, you don't need to worry about me lecturing you here. In fact, cards on the table, when my body was recovering from cancer and I was trying to put weight back on, I used to sit down and have a box — not one, but one *box* — of ice creams for dessert. No person who has done that in their life is in a position to tell you about healthy eating.

I like food. I like healthy food and I like unhealthy food. I like them both for different reasons. I like healthy food because it feels good to eat, knowing I'm doing the right thing for my body. I like unhealthy food because I'm human. We're hardwired to like unhealthy food, so that's not changing any time soon.

The tuck shop at my old school owes its survival from 2011–15 almost exclusively to me and the mind-blowing quantities of chicken, cranberry and brie paninis, chocolate muffins with a liquid caramel centre, nacho toasties and strudels which I consumed throughout my schooling. As I noted before, this had its impact on me. I was never particularly overweight, but the unhealthy food I piled in nonstop, combined with the complete absence of any exercise, meant I was a bit chubby, which wasn't ideal, given the health implications of being above a healthy weight. But that's before we even get into the mental impact of the actual food I was consuming.

The impact of what you eat on your mental health and well-being (and therefore your resilience) is just unbelievable. Get a load of this: all of the following have been linked to adolescents eating unhealthy food:

- aggression
- ADHD
- poor concentration
- lowered immunity
- delayed brain development (particularly with high-fat and high-sugar diets)
- worse memory and information retention
- depression and anxiety.

The opposite is also true as well: healthy and nutritious diets reduce the risk of all of the above.

I realised at the time that a lot of the food I ate was unhealthy — high in calories, low in nutrients — but I definitely don't think I knew the exact impact, or if I had been told, I certainly didn't believe it. That's something which might have possibly, maybe, changed a little of the way I ate. I wouldn't have been rushing to trade in my second muffin of the day for a salad, but hey, maybe I wouldn't have been having the second muffin of the day at all.

I look back now pretty surprised about how awful the food we all ate as teenagers really was. Sure, I still eat unhealthy food now, like I said — plenty of it, to be honest. My diet now is healthy, but with unhealthy things thrown in, whereas previously it used to be unhealthy with healthy things thrown in almost by accident.

It sounds like a minor and wishy-washy kind of difference, but I think in practice this is the easier thing to strive towards as a teen: eat a healthy diet where possible (because many of those impacts described above stem from a lack of good food rather than too much bad food), throw in some bad food when you want but keep it reasonable, and exercise enough that you can justify doing so.

## Alcohol

You know about alcohol already, right? Depending on the wide range of experiences you'll have across your teenage years, you could currently be anywhere between having tried a sip of Dad's beer once and wincing, through to at the other end of the scale, currently drinking regularly — legally or otherwise. But no matter what stage you're at, you'll see adverts for it all over the place, and your drunk relatives at Christmas, and you'll certainly, if you haven't already, get one hell of a talking-to about it at school.

Once again, I'm not one to tell you what to do — when I was a teenager I certainly had my own pretty varied range of drinking experiences. In year 13 in particular, before I was diagnosed with cancer, I was drinking a lot. There's probably not anything someone could have said to me to change my habits back then, and you might feel the same way. But I think that, especially coming from someone who has walked that path, it's worth me sharing some science around the effects of alcohol consumption by young people which I've only learnt since getting into the work I do now, and which you might want to take into account when making your own decisions. Most of this information comes from neuroscientist Nathan Wallis, as this is one of those areas he specialises in.

It's undeniable science that the impact of alcohol on your brain before you're about eighteen is pretty huge. Here are some facts:

- In the vast majority of cases, those who drink even moderate amounts of alcohol before the age of eighteen have measurably less developed brains and lower IQs in their forties. To spell this out, what I'm saying is that *people who drink before they're eighteen are almost certain to be less intelligent throughout the rest of their life than they would have been otherwise.*
- *The amount you drink* corresponds to the level of damage and reduction in intelligence.
- *The earlier you start drinking* corresponds to the level of damage and reduction in intelligence.

This means that, taking myself, for example, I've literally deprived my brain of development it would've had had I not been drinking when I was a teen. My brain is measurably less developed, and therefore I am less intelligent, than someone who didn't start drinking until they were older, or drank less, or didn't drink at all.

Current research suggests that teenage brains, which are still growing and developing, can only handle about one unit of alcohol an hour before damage starts to occur (remembering that one unit is roughly one small glass of wine, a can of mid-strength beer, or less than a can of most RTDs). After the brain has finished developing — generally by eighteen, but as late as into the twenties for some people — it can handle far more without suffering this damage.

The damage occurs in a couple of parts of the brain: firstly, the hippocampus, which is responsible for memory. This is pretty clear from the science: its level of development correlates to the age at which the person first went over the threshold of one drink per hour. Those who waited until they were older than eighteen are the only people that have a fully developed, full-size hippocampus. And the size of the hippocampus correlates directly to the strength and ability of your memory.

Secondly, it's been shown to damage a part of the brain called the prefrontal cortex, which I described in chapter 5 as the 'solution-finding, problem-solving' part of your brain. Or, as Nathan Wallis puts it, the part of the brain responsible for everything you can do but your dog can't. Eat food? Go for a run? You and the dog can both do that. Feel happy? You and the dog can both do that, too. Read this paragraph and make sense of it? You've got your prefrontal cortex to thank for that. Setting goals? Prefrontal cortex. Planning to achieve those goals? Prefrontal cortex.

Drinking before the age of eighteen impacts its ability to

develop and function — which, to put it simply, reduces your capability to do more than your dog.

In summary, if you want your brain to develop to its full potential, you need to either not drink at all before you're eighteen or, being practical, learn to nurse each drink for an hour, or split up your drinks with water in between. You don't have to not go to parties or not drink at all — you just need to drink fairly slowly. Then, according to the current research, once you're over about eighteen, you can take your perfectly developed and pristine brain into adult life.

In summary, the damage you do to your brain by drinking isn't done at university, it's done at high school. Interesting, right?

.........

It's not always that easy, though, is it? There are two big things about our drinking culture here in New Zealand: firstly, the normalisation of alcohol and drinking, and secondly, peer pressure.

The normalisation element of our drinking culture can be hard to wrap your head fully around without having the benefit of another culture to compare it to. Take my word for it, though — New Zealand's drinking is in a realm of its own, and not in a good way. For instance, in parts of Europe, if you survey a group and ask how many drinks it's socially acceptable to have on a night out, the average answer is three. Ask that same question in New Zealand and the answer is thirteen. Quite a discrepancy there!

Also, for comparison, alcohol cannot legally be sold in supermarkets in Australia, only in bottle shops. The Australians, despite having one hell of a drinking culture themselves, find the idea of alcohol being sold in supermarkets completely foreign. It's an interesting example of international contrast in our perception of alcohol from even a young age.

When I was a teenager, alcohol was commonplace. It was just a part of my world, and the world around me. To question the safety of alcohol would have been like questioning the safety of tomato sauce, or cell phones, or anything else that was an everyday part of life. I never saw it as a danger, certainly never as a drug. It was 'just' alcohol. I think this normalisation of alcohol in our culture contributed to my drinking, at least in the early stages.

I'm not your mum. I'm not going to tell you that it's all terrible and wrong and very, very bad. I get it: maybe you want to go to parties and drink heaps, to be part of that culture and that experience, because that's what I wanted and it's certainly what I did. What am I going to do — tell you that after doing it myself, you can't?

What I do want you to know, however, is that while it's fine if you want to do that, you need to know that, generally, the way New Zealand drinks is not normal. Everyone else at the party might be doing it, but it's not normal. You might have been around it or seen it since you were a kid, but it's not normal. Even if your parents or role models are doing it, it's still not normal. It's not what other young people, or adults for that matter, are doing virtually anywhere else in the world. It's not normal to make yourself sick or wake up hungover, or in hospital, or lying in some bushes. I didn't know that at the time, but I think you ought to.

Chlöe Swarbrick has an interesting take on New Zealand's binge-drinking culture and how she believes honesty and open discussion is the way to bring about change:

> 'I think it's really important for us to recognise that anybody who is put out there as supposedly successful in life is never totally perfect or untainted, and so when it comes to alcohol and abuse thereof, I've thought that it's been really important to be open about that because of that reality of showing people who I am — with all my flaws.
>
> 'That personal experience was effectively an attempt to self-medicate, for lack of a better term, with some really dark and trying times when I didn't have the language or the support systems to reach out and ask for help.
>
> 'Because of our culture where excessive drinking is not only normalised, but I would say glamorised, we have a situation where younger people find it very easy to mask their problems by engaging in excessive drinking.
>
> 'We have a culture which encourages you to drink if you're having a good day, if you're having a bad day, or if you're just having a day — and that's not positive. There are massive mental-health repercussions for that, but you can also end up unintentionally fostering some quite harmful social relationships if they're entirely based on drinking. I think the fact that sits unchallenged can be quite dangerous, and so I think in just trying to offer all of the sides of my experiences and trying to not just present this Instagram-curated version of what I am means that there's the opportunity for more people to join into and have those conversations.'

The second part of this is peer pressure. There are two types of peer pressure, and one of them very much relates to the normalisation mentioned above. The first type, which I'll call unintentional, stems from a sense of expectation to conform to the societal norms. No one tells you that you have to do it, no one laughs and points like in those comics in your health-class book. (I seriously remember one health class, doing some absurd role play where we had to act out how we would turn down a drink if someone offered it to us, which was hilarious at the time and even funnier to look back on now.) It's just that it's the norm, and so you feel like you ought to partake as well.

The second type of peer pressure is intentional — you might not get pointed and laughed at, but your mates might say, 'Go on, have another' or 'Jeez, you're a bit slow' when you've been nursing a drink or, 'I need a teammate for beer pong, you're up'.

By the way, these examples are what's really meant by peer pressure — not someone giving you shit if you don't drink. Peer pressure is normally either:

1. Unspoken but perceived and often without pressure, like the unintentional example above, or
2. Just conversational, like the intentional example above.

The term 'pressure' is a bit deceptive — it's more just a natural flow of things in an environment where drinking plenty is the norm — like a mate grabbing you another drink while they're up out of good intentions and you feeling like it's polite to drink it.

Both these kinds of pressure can be challenging to overcome at times. All I can say is that you need to be strong and confident enough in yourself to be able to feel solid in your decisions around alcohol, whatever those might be. If a certain level of tolerance, and then some gentle ribbing in return, doesn't make people back off, then you're probably not surrounded by the right people.

••••••••

So then, after all that chat, what's the answer? No alcohol until eighteen? Twenty-one? Some alcohol, but only on weekends? More alcohol, but less frequently? Less alcohol, but more frequently? What does that choice mean at parties? Bring a few drinks and nurse them? Bring non-alcoholic drinks and face getting hassled? Stay completely sober?

The truth is that whatever the answer is for you is your own choice. Once again, I'm not your mum. Although, on that note, the choice you make may inevitably have a bit of input from your parents, for as long as you're under their roof. Maybe they'll be pretty chill and leave the choice to you, maybe they'll make that choice for you entirely; hopefully they'll listen to you and allow you to have some input. The reality is that even when your parents have input or believe that they've made a choice for you, *the choice still remains yours*.

Interestingly, as Nathan Wallis told me, research shows that when parents are entirely opposed to their teen consuming any alcohol and prohibit it altogether, the teen may hide their alcohol consumption, which can lead to worse outcomes than for parents who discuss and negotiate the amount of alcohol consumed. The teens with the lowest levels of harm are those whose parents reach agreement with them on what is acceptable.

Regardless, and while the final decision remains yours, there are two things which you ought to aim for when making that choice: delaying and moderation.

- Delaying, because the research is pretty unequivocal that if you start drinking before the age of eighteen (more than one unit per hour), your brain development is going to be stunted, and that's the end of it. If you can hold off another six months, or a year, or until you're eighteen, you are squeezing out every little bit of growth and development you can, which will make a real impact throughout your life.
- Moderation, particularly if you do decide to start drinking before you're eighteen. Sure, a night out where you have five drinks over four hours isn't perfect, but it's a hell of a lot better for your brain than a night out where you have twelve drinks over four hours. A Saturday once a month where you have a few beers is going to be better for you than a month where you have six drinks every Saturday without fail.

I know these goals pretty quickly come under fire when you apply them to the real world. I'm not deluded about the fact it's a hell of a lot harder than just saying 'wait a few years, and don't have too much'.

Looking back now, and trying to figure out what would have helped me to be a bit more moderate with my drinking when I was at high school, I think having another goal or a purpose to draw my focus away from partying would have been a major factor. Being involved in sport is a big one which comes to mind. If I had a goal I was striving towards in sport, then I think I would've been, at least in some part, turned away from alcohol by the effects it would've had on my physical performance.

Thinking about your purpose can also give you the strength to not go off the deep end when really tough times strike. When I talked to Liam Malone about how he spiralled a bit after his mum's passing, he echoed a similar thought about how a purpose would have minimised some of the less healthy parts of his lifestyle.

> 'I was binge drinking and living a very unhealthy lifestyle. Maybe doing those things is just a part of growing up in New Zealand, but when you do them during a time of great adversity and suffering, it magnifies the negative outcomes of going through an event like that. I think that if I'd had something at that point in time which I was really passionate about and a vision of myself that I could work towards, I think things would have been very different, because I just would have had a healthier lifestyle.'

If you can find something to aspire towards, be that fitness or health, a team, a study goal, a result, anything which can be improved by you not drinking, then you've got something to weigh up when considering the choice of 'do I drink or not?'

## Summary

That's it, it's done. I'm not going to tell you any more about how much you're supposed to run and not stay up late and not eat bad food or drink too much. The bottom line, though, and the reason it was essential to mention this stuff, is that it all plays a big role in your wellbeing and therefore your resilience. You don't have to overthink it — just take it from me, someone who used to do all of these things badly and now does them slightly better. I feel better for it.

I don't think you can be fully resilient without moving towards being better at all of these things. The steps you take don't have to be major — they can be very small — but just taking gradual steps in the right direction will benefit you when you face adversity.

# OUTRO: STAND YOUR GROUND

So, that's it really. Well, that's certainly everything that going through cancer has taught me about resilience. It's also everything I've dedicated the last nine years of my life to learning, teaching and presenting. It's all the mistakes I made, lessons I learnt, changes I would make if I went through my teen years again. It's everything I've learnt from the incredible people who I've walked alongside and interviewed for the book. It's all I've got for you.

The last few years of working and presenting, particularly at schools, has been really interesting for me — because I'm young enough to have been in the position of the audience not that many years ago, and yet now I'm apparently old enough to have the privilege of being the person up the front. We had some brilliant guest speakers when I was at school, and they presented exceptionally well, but to be honest I don't think I retained any lessons that they were trying to impart to me — which is no reflection on them, but rather, probably a reflection on me as a listener. And so now, with the roles reversed, I'd be pretty hypocritical to feel bad if the students I present to don't retain all, some, or any of the information I've given them. I'm perfectly satisfied walking away knowing that, hopefully, some of them will retain something which benefits them in some positive way at some point in the future. That's all I could ever ask for, and it's truly a privilege for me to even have that opportunity.

In a sense, writing the conclusion to this book feels a bit the same. I didn't read a book like this in my teen years, because I never had the opportunity — books like this didn't exist. But also, to be honest, I don't think I would've been as driven or forward-focused as you must have been to pick up this book and read it.

Like I said at the start:

> Hopefully, there will be a line or two which will make it worth the time you spent sifting through these pages — something that really hits home for you, and makes you think differently, and helps you to become more resilient.

Hopefully, this has been the case, and even if it's not something which has a profound impact on you now, hopefully it has planted a seed of something which goes on to benefit you in the future — perhaps when that inevitable adversity that lies ahead rears its head and enters your life, as it will for all of us at some point.

In this book, you've read about the four Ss: Slow Down, Salvage, Streamline and Stand Alongside. Those Ss are tangible and straightforward actions, a framework to take into life: try to do this, and not do that. This is intentional. I speak to a huge range of people about resilience, from all walks of life and a range of ages. They've got different attitudes, opinions and life experiences which have shaped them. They are facing different challenges and reacting in different ways. I usually have a very limited amount of time to speak to them — a tiny window in which to try to give them something useful that they can latch on to. That's why I keep it as simple as possible, with the Four Ss: simple, short, sharp actions to take.

I suppose, if there were an end result or a product which I wanted you to come away with, it would be a fifth S: the ability to Stand Your Ground — my term for what I feel is the attitude of optimism you can take into adversity and suffering.

The good news is that, through working your way through the first four Ss, *you already have the fifth S*. A sense of self-confidence or defiance in the face of adversity is within you now. The fifth S is the creation, the sum, the product of you putting the first four Ss into practice.

Maybe you might not feel it yet, but when you next come up against adversity, and you apply some of the lessons of this book, and you're able to pass safely through challenges which previously would have knocked you down, you will grow in confidence. That is the fifth S.

Resilience is what allows you to Stand Your Ground, and not back down in the face of adversity. In turn, Standing Your

Ground in the face of adversity grows your resilience even further. Standing Your Ground can be summed up by the term 'confident defiance' — having the guts to face the challenge; to acknowledge its significance, and still to push back.

Let me share with you part of a speech I once gave at a big event in Sydney:

> On that first night in the BMTU, after I was diagnosed, I lay there by myself, in a half slumber, in a foreign place, surrounded by complete strangers. As I lay there, I did not wish to live. Instead, I wished that if this was going to be the thing that killed me, that I wanted to face it with strength. If it was going to kill me, it would do so on my terms. I did not want to let fear dictate my death any more than it had my life.

This is probably the earliest example of the fifth S in action in my own personal story, the first time I consciously decided to face up to adversity and control my reaction to it, rather than letting it control me.

When facing adversity, be it minor or massive, there are often these moments of choice where you are presented with the opportunity to either take what is happening lying down, letting it define or control you, or to Stand Your Ground — put up some resistance and not just accept defeat. It's about refusing to roll over and submit to the circumstances you find yourself in. It is to make a conscious decision to *choose to not let yourself be broken by adversity*. At moments when you're faced with giving in and Standing Your Ground, you can *consciously choose to face adversity with defiance and the resolve to beat it*, not with the acceptance that it will beat you. This is only possible, however, when you are confident that you have resilience skills and believe in your ability to put them to work.

.........

I don't think there's actually a word in the English language which captures exactly the attitude I'm trying to convey here — but fortunately, we're not limited to the English language to express these concepts. Take German, for example — they have all kinds of handy words for specific situations you're trying to describe (like *Verschlimmbesserung*, for when you're trying to improve a bad situation but only end up buggering it up even worse). The word I think really captures this idea I'm expressing is, thankfully, a whole lot easier to spell. It's *Sisu*.

Sisu is a Finnish word (as in, from Finland) that Finns (as in, people from Finland) use to describe their national character. It's best defined as, well, what I'm talking about: a sustained attitude comprised of courage, bravery, determination, perseverance and resilience in the face of adversity where success isn't all that likely. It is close to what we might call 'grit', or 'guts', but it's more than that — it's a sense of proud resolve in not wanting to give in to failure or defeat by adversity, wanting to win out over it instead. It is resolving to overcome the difficult or apparently impossible head on, doing whatever needs to be done to get through, and persevering even when others would give up or change course, whilst maintaining dignity and focus. It is going about this suffering and perseverance in a quiet and unassuming way throughout, without crying out or relenting. It is the ability to suffer and remain stoic in the face of that suffering. It's awesome. It could, in fact, be the fifth S.

In recent years, thinking *similar* to this has fallen out of favour — and quite rightly. I want to make it quite clear, however, that what I am suggesting is not the good old Kiwi attitude of 'harden up', and 'get over it', or saying that the best way to deal with adversity is to ignore it — *which it is not*. This has been the prevalent attitude for a long time — keeping a stiff upper lip, bottling it all up inside, carrying on like nothing is wrong. People weren't encouraged to share their feelings and challenges. When I was at school, kids would be completely covert about going to the guidance counsellor, because if it was known that you were seeing a counsellor you'd be signing up for getting a whole lot of shit about it. Among friends, especially with guys, showing your emotions was often discouraged. You were generally told to just get over it.

If you're a bit younger, hopefully it's hard to picture this being the reality only ten years or so ago, but believe me, talking about how you felt or admitting you were struggling was pretty rare. Consequently, no surprises, we as a country have truly mind-blowingly bad statistics around mental-health issues and suicide.

Thankfully, things have changed. In the time I've been working with schools and companies on resilience, nine years or so now, this attitude has flipped an entire 180 degrees: now, some of the companies I work with have emotion-sharing in meetings, tools and strategies to help people communicate their feelings more effectively, and in-office psychologists. Schools have a massive focus on mental health and wellbeing in general — through education, support and in their school culture. I said before that books like this didn't exist when I was your age — because basically, there just wasn't a market for them. So this book is itself a product of this huge societal change in how we learn about, educate, discuss and interact with wellbeing. Now, we're encouraged not to hold our emotions in or hide them, or pretend things are okay when they're not: we talk about our feelings and share them, we talk about our problems, and we have reaped some rewards as a society for doing so.

Obviously, I'm all for that, and that's why there's a whole S for it: Stand Alongside. I know myself just how critical it is to lean on other people when overcoming adversity, and that means sharing your struggles and your emotions with them openly and honestly.

So, to make it explicitly clear, Standing Your Ground doesn't mean hiding your emotions from others or yourself. It is not pretending problems don't exist, or that adversity doesn't impact you, or trying to act like you don't feel scared or angry or afraid or sad in the face of serious challenges. It's the absolute opposite: it is in fact acknowledging all of these things, accepting them, and then choosing to be defiant in the face of them. It is *Sisu*.

.........

When I was growing up, my mum always talked to me about the importance of being able to 'sit with the suffering'. In essence, it's quite similar to Standing Your Ground, but the key difference is that Standing Your Ground is active, while sitting with the suffering is passive. I know what she meant — that sometimes you just have to acknowledge that things suck, but that it will pass — but I feel you should take it one step further. Rather than just sitting with suffering, you should be taking active steps to mitigate or prevent that suffering, or to deal with overcoming the adversity causing the suffering.

At their core, both these ideas are about accepting and acknowledging situations in which you have no other alternative than facing up to the adversity ahead of you and the emotion which comes with that. Both are about trying to not squirm and escape and hide from tough times and tough feelings. But while sitting with the suffering is about just battening down the hatches and trying to survive, Standing Your Ground is about actively employing an attitude which seeks to fight back and overcome, to engage with your adversity and push back on it.

When I was in hospital, I used to have moments where I would mock and taunt my cancer, particularly once I appeared to have the upper hand in the fight. This wasn't so much a direct conversation with my cancer as it was with my situation as a whole. I used to take the predicament and try to do my best *just to spite it*: I would be as positive, as optimistic, as happy, as healthy as possible *just to stop it from thinking it had beaten me.*

I think you have to feel this emotion to be able to Stand Your Ground fully. The desire to win, to beat the adversity, is what drives this attitude. I've found that one of the best ways to find this emotion is to view adversity through the lens of a personal slight. It's not about taking everything personally or feeling that everything that goes wrong is a disaster afflicting only you (taking a 'why me?' attitude), but rather seeing the challenge itself as a personal attack on your resilience. Taking my cancer again as an example, I never asked, 'Why me?', nor wished the situation was different — but I did accept that since this was the situation I was in, I wanted to beat it and overcome it. I was not pissed off at life; in fact, I was more grateful for life than ever, but I had a form of controlled 'pissed off' which I channelled into energy and effort to fight with. When I was at my lowest, I knew it was up to me to beat the adversity I was facing. I was defiant. I refused to be weak in its face. I would not just lie down and get steamrolled by adversity.

There's a good chance I sound nuts right now. Sometimes, when I talk about this, audiences look at me like I'm a bit crazy. But trust me on this, it was incredibly powerful in my story and, far more importantly than that, I've met people who have applied this S to their own adversities of many different kinds and reaped the rewards, and others who have not done so and were far more easily broken by challenges. There's a hell of a lot to resilience, far more than what's in this book, but at least a small part of resilience is *having some bloody fight in you*. That is the core of Standing Your Ground and, hopefully, the product of learning the four Ss in this book.

Resilience is not 'hardening up'. It's not 'taking a concrete pill' or 'getting over it' either. It's incredibly nuanced and composed of a whole range of factors, knowledge, experiences, learnings and skills. But part of it is definitely not lying down and accepting defeat when things go wrong, or becoming bogged down in your feelings, or giving in to challenges. Once you give away your only real control during tough times — your attitude and effort to be resilient — you're a small ship in a big storm. Standing Your Ground is about actually fighting back, keeping a grip on the rudder, regardless of how big the storm is and how little impact you think you can have on the direction you're going in.

It's also worth making clear that when it comes to this attitude of Standing Your Ground and facing adversity with confident defiance, this is about *an overall or big-picture approach*, not necessarily on a minute-by-minute level. I know as well as everyone else that sometimes it just feels good to feel shit, to rant and moan and whine and whinge about things, whether they're big or small. We all have those moments. Standing Your Ground is about your overall attitude — and the outcome for someone who likes to have an occasional whinge, but deep down knows they can overcome anything, is going to be a hell of a lot better than someone who keeps trucking along in silence but doesn't back themselves to be able to overcome the challenges life throws at them. You're still allowed to have a moan sometimes, as long as it doesn't change your overall feeling towards or response to the adversity you're facing.

In hospital, I would have moments when I would drop my attempt at confident defiance, at standing my ground. Usually it was when I was in the shower. I was so weak and sick and tired that I could barely stand up, and sometimes I couldn't, so the nurses had to put a seat in the shower for me. Once I passed out from exhaustion and the heat and hit my head on the floor.

Each time I showered, which I could only cope with every third day or so, I had to confront the full, naked extent of the havoc chemo was wreaking on my body. My ribs were jutting out from my sides, and my ankles were so thin I could wrap my thumb and forefinger around them. I would face myself in the mirror and not recognise my bald head, missing eyebrows and eyelashes, sunken eyes. Because of all this, showers were always a low point, but they were also a private time, so I would stand under the water and take stock of just how shitty this all was and the strife I was in. There, secluded from my adversity and hidden from sight, I would acknowledge that this was bad and I was sick of it. Sometimes I'd feel a bit sorry for myself, sometimes I would feel sad. Then, I would get out, dry off, get back in my hospital gown and bed, and put my brave face, my confident defiance, back on, as I stared the adversity down once more.

That willingness to accept my negative emotions, to choose to control them instead of letting them control me, gave me pride, and a tiny piece of power, in my battle with adversity.

.........

I think the reason that adopting this attitude works is that often, if not always, the negative impacts that we perceive to have come from adversity, be it minor or major, stem not from the adversity itself *but the thoughts we have and the emotions we attach to the adversity*. Often, it is our reaction to the problem — our fear, our sadness, our desperation to escape it, and our inability or unwillingness to deal with these emotions and feelings — which heightens our response and makes us feel even worse than the problem itself does.

If we resolve to spite the adversity, by keeping our emotions as positive as possible, to not allow the adversity to crush us or break us by making us feel these things, then we are less affected by the adversity itself. So much of our suffering often comes not from the act or the event of adversity itself, but how it makes us feel, and if we can change how it makes us feel then we need not worry about the event.

Emotions aren't bad, feeling emotions isn't bad, recognising or acknowledging these emotions isn't bad. But the impacts of these emotions can be bad if we're not able to control our interactions with them. It creates new problems which come from not being able to face them, or running away from them. I've talked earlier about the idea of escapism, and the issues it brings when people choose to hide from, or mask, or numb the emotions which come from adversity. Hopefully, you come away from this book not only with a greater knowledge of what it means to be resilient, but with an understanding of just how critical it is to not hide from your negative emotions or be afraid of them. Not only will it rob you of opportunities, like taking a chance on a relationship, or following a dream, or trying to achieve something big, but it will leave you in perpetual fear.

We know that challenges lie ahead — this inevitable adversity. We know that bad times are unavoidable. If you can't overcome or face or handle or sit with adversity and the negative emotions it brings, then you have plenty to fear in the future, because no matter how much you might want it to be untrue, there is adversity lurking ahead of you. On the other hand, if you don't fear negative emotions, you don't have to fear adversity, and as such you have limitless possibilities ahead of you — you can take chances, take risks, and not be afraid of the outcomes and the tough emotions they may possibly bring.

This is the point you should be ready to move into, gradually, if you are not already there. After these pages, and these Ss, and these stories and bits of advice from people who have faced all forms of adversity and gone on to achieve all forms of success, I hope you feel prepared and ready to face adversity with a new set of tools and skills to apply, and with a new sense of confidence — better prepared for life, and the things it is going to throw at you.

With this sense of preparedness should come the final S, the outward appearance in which all of these other skills and tools are wrapped: confident defiance, the bravery to stare down adversity and not want to run away or hide from the emotion it brings. The power to Stand Your Ground.

But if not, then there is something I would wish you to remember — one thing that I hope would give you the same spark, the same energy to go out into the world as that sense of resilience would. And it would be very simple.

When I ended up in hospital, sitting between child and adult in the eyes of the medical system, I had a number of procedures done in the children's ward: CHOC, the place I spoke of meeting Kane earlier. And whilst when I arrived onto the BMTU where I had most of my treatment, I was surrounded by people who looked exactly like I expected them to look — old and grey people, like my grandparents, three or four times my own age — when I went into CHOC, things were different. To my complete shock, in CHOC I was surrounded by young people. Young people who probably look a hell of a lot like you, young people who probably *are* a hell of a lot like you. That ward was full of teenagers, high-school students, and even younger kids. Young people with hopes and dreams and goals and ambitions for the future, just as real and vivid as yours and mine are.

I'm not sure if I was stupid, or perhaps I was just a more sheltered, more naïve, less worldly teenager than most, but I truly did not know, until the moment I walked into the ward and saw it with my own eyes, that just up the road from me, at all times, there had always been a ward full of young people dying of cancer. Young people, many of whom, through no fault of their own, had their light snuffed out prematurely. Who did not get to go on living and chasing those dreams, goals, ambitions. Every day, of every year, at all times, young people were engaged in this perpetual fight to survive and to get back out into the world — to have the chance at living life.

I was one of the lucky ones who walked out of that place — and there were many who did not. And as a direct result of that, ever since, I've felt a sense of responsibility to go on and live my life to the fullest, to do everything I possibly can, on behalf of those people who no longer have the opportunity. Because I know that, had the roles been reversed and I didn't walk out of there, all I would have wanted, all I could've asked, would be for the person who *was* lucky enough to get out of there to give it 100 per cent effort on my behalf. To take risks, to push boundaries, to give it absolute hell — for me.

Hopefully, now you understand why I feel this responsibility, and this privilege, on my shoulders, right? It's not fair for me to have taken someone else's spot, then to go and do only average, go and give it only a half-decent attempt, when someone else might have done better. I don't think that's an unreasonable thing to feel.

But the thing is, it's not my responsibility alone, because . . . well, why would it be? Logically, why? Is it my responsibility because I met these people? Is it my responsibility because I saw this place? Is it my responsibility because I had a whole heap of money invested in me by our healthcare system?

I don't think any of these reasons make sense. I think that, actually, it's a collective responsibility we all share as young people — to go out and to live life to the fullest, on behalf of those other young people who don't get the opportunity to do so. Because that is really all I would've asked. I'm sure that's all Kane would have asked, too. Not for anyone to feel sorry for him, not to feel guilty that we are still here — but just to get out there and do stuff, give it a nudge, simply because *we are lucky to be able to do so.*

I didn't understand that part — how lucky I was to have the opportunity to be alive — until I saw first-hand those people who did not, and risked becoming one of them. My hope for you is that you can take away this knowledge without having to see it with your own eyes.

And hopefully now, armed with these skills and tools of resilience, you'll be better placed to be able to go out and achieve things, make things happen, make an impact, no matter what adversity you face. It's the least we can do.

# ACKNOWLEDGEMENTS

This book took the long way to get here — and in the process, I can confirm it has made at least one person more resilient. It also means there's a great number of people to whom I owe the credit.

Firstly, the incredible team who got it to the point it is in your hands now: Krysana Hanley, Leanne McGregor, Abba Renshaw, Grace Wang, Katrina Duncan, Mike Wagg and Tracey Lowndes. Michelle Hurley, you are a champion. Working with you and your brilliant team at Allen & Unwin has been some of the best 'salvaging' I've ever had the fortune of experiencing. From the moment I got on that first call with you, I knew that this book had found its home. Sarah Ell, who took 100,000 words of rambling yarns and made it into a beautiful manuscript. Tracey Wogan, who took that manuscript and made it into a book. You both did such an extraordinary job of understanding not only what I wanted to say, but how I wanted to say it. Thank you for carrying this book forward with your immense talent and wisdom.

Then, to my family — for being the source of so much of whatever I've learnt about resilience, and the core of whatever resilience I have. My partner Jem, for being an honest sounding board, and for so stoically tolerating my many and prolonged absences over the past nine years as I've lived out the work in this book — thank you for being so resilient. My parents and my families — for being my first and defining source of support and guidance in my life. I feel so lucky to have you all and to have learnt from you all. My nana, for showing me that even when things have fallen apart, again, you can pick them up and move forward with a smile on your face and a prevailing attitude of optimism, once you've put the jug on. Your resilience, and your attitude towards life, continue to inspire me ten years on.

To the interviewees and those who contributed to this book, both through formal interviews and casual chats alike — I hope that this has been an opportunity to take something good from the bad by using your adversity to benefit others. I'm humbled that so many of you made yourselves vulnerable and shared not only what the highs have taught you, but also the lows.

To Kane, Dee and your family, for so kindly allowing me to share your story. Kane, your legacy continues to live on.

Finally, to all those I've had the privilege of presenting to over the last nine years. Granted, you've usually not had much of a say in it — most of you have shown up to your school hall or company conference and been subjected to me for an hour or two. But nonetheless, it has been such an immense honour to share my story, what I've learnt, and my work with you all. To those of you who have so kindly reciprocated and shared your own stories with me, you've taught me much of the practical applications for the Four S Model within this book, and have helped others through doing so.

AUTHOR PHOTOGRAPH BY FRANCINE BOER